PATHWAYS

Listening, Speaking, and Critical Thinking

3A

Becky Tarver Chase
Kristin L. Johannsen

Rolling green hills in Washington state, USA.

Australia • Brazil • Japan • Korea • Mexico • Singapore • Spain • United Kingdom • United States

Pathways Split Text 3A
Listening, Speaking, and Critical Thinking
Becky Tarver Chase
Kristin L. Johannsen

Regional Director, Asia ELT/School:
Michael Cahill

Publisher, Asia ELT/School: Edward Yoshioka

Regional Manager, Production & Rights:
Pauline Lim

Senior Production Executive: Cindy Chai

Publisher: Sherrise Roehr

Executive Editor: Laura Le Dréan

Acquisitions Editor: Tom Jefferies

Senior Development Editor:
Mary Whittemore

Director of Global Marketing: Ian Martin

Director of U.S. Marketing: Jim McDonough

Marketing Manager: Caitlin Driscoll

Marketing Manager: Katie Kelley

Marketing Coordinator: Jide Iruka

Director of Content and Media Production:
Michael Burggren

Content Project Manager: Daisy Sosa

Manufacturing Manager: Marcia Locke

Manufacturing Buyer: Marybeth Hennebury

Production Intern: Geena Hillman

Cover Design: Page 2 LLC

Cover Image: Terry W. Eggers/CORBIS

Interior Design: Page 2 LLC

Composition: Nesbitt Graphics, Inc.

© 2013 National Geographic Learning, a part of Cengage Learning

ALL RIGHTS RESERVED. No part of this work covered by the copyright herein may be reproduced, transmitted, stored or used in any form or by any means graphic, electronic, or mechanical, including but not limited to photocopying, recording, scanning, digitizing, taping, Web distribution, information networks, or information storage and retrieval systems, except as permitted under Section 107 or 108 of the 1976 United States Copyright Act, without the prior written permission of the publisher.

> For product information and technology assistance, contact us at
> **Cengage Learning Asia Customer Support, 65-6410-1200**
> For permission to use material from this text or product,
> submit all requests online at **www.cengageasia.com/permissions**
> Further permissions questions can be emailed to
> **asia.permissionrequest@cengage.com**

ISBN 13: 978-1-285-15976-8
ISBN 10: 1-285-15976-4

Cengage Learning Asia Pte Ltd
151 Lorong Chuan #02-08
New Tech Park
Singapore 556741

National Geographic Learning
20 Channel Center St.
Boston, MA 02210
USA

Cengage Learning is a leading provider of customized learning solutions with office locations around the globe, including Andover, Melbourne, Mexico City, Stamford (CT), Toronto, Hong Kong, New Delhi, Seoul, Singapore, and Tokyo. Locate your local office at **www.cengage.com/global**

Cengage Learning products are represented in Canada by Nelson Education, Ltd.

Visit National Geographic Learning online at **ngl.cengage.com**
For product information, visit our website at **www.cengageasia.com**

Printed in Singapore
3 4 5 6 7 17 16 15

ACKNOWLEDGMENTS

The authors and publisher would like to thank the following reviewers:

UNITED STATES **Adrianne Aiko Thompson**, Miami Dade College, Miami, Florida; **Gokhan Alkanat**, Auburn University at Montgomery, Alabama; **Nikki Ashcraft**, Shenandoah University, Virginia; **Karin Avila-John**, University of Dayton, Ohio; **Shirley Baker**, Alliant International University, California; **John Baker**, Oakland Community College, Michigan; **Evina Baquiran Torres**, Zoni Language Centers, New York; **Michelle Bell**, University of South Florida, Florida; **Nancy Boyer**, Golden West College, California; **Carol Brutza**, Gateway Community College, Connecticut; **Sarah Camp**, University of Kentucky, Center for ESL, Kentucky; **Maria Caratini**, Eastfield College, Texas; **Ana Maria Cepero**, Miami Dade College, Florida; **Daniel Chaboya**, Tulsa Community College, Oklahoma; **Patricia Chukwueke**, English Language Institute – UCSD Extension, California; **Julia A. Correia**, Henderson State University, Connecticut; **Suzanne Crisci**, Bunker Hill Community College, Massachusetts; **Katie Crowder**, University of North Texas, Texas; **Lynda Dalgish**, Concordia College, New York; **Jeffrey Diluglio**, Center for English Language and Orientation Programs: Boston University, Massachusetts; **Tim DiMatteo**, Southern New Hampshire University, New Hampshire; **Scott Dirks**, Kaplan International Center at Harvard Square, Massachusetts; **Margo Downey**, Center for English Language and Orientation Programs: Boston University, Massachusetts; **John Drezek**, Richland College, Texas; **Anwar El-Issa**, Antelope Valley College, California; **Anrisa Fannin**, The International Education Center at Diablo Valley College, California; **Jennie Farnell**, University of Connecticut, American Language Program, Connecticut; **Mark Fisher**, Lone Star College, Texas; **Celeste Flowers**, University of Central Arkansas, Arkansas; **John Fox**, English Language Institute, Georgia; **Pradel R. Frank**, Miami Dade College, Florida; **Sally Gearheart**, Santa Rosa Jr. College, California; **Karen Grubbs**, ELS Language Centers, Florida; **Joni Hagigeorges**, Salem State University, Massachusetts; **Valerie Heming**, University of Central Missouri, Missouri; **Mary Hill**, North Shore Community College, Massachusetts; **Harry L. Holden**, North Lake College, Texas; **Ingrid Holm**, University of Massachusetts Amherst, Massachusetts; **Marianne Hsu Santelli**, Middlesex County College, New Jersey; **Katie Hurter**, Lone Star College – North Harris, Texas; **Justin Jernigan**, Georgia Gwinnett College, Georgia; **Barbara A. Jonckheere**, American Language Institute at California State University, Long Beach, California; **Susan Jordan**, Fisher College, Massachusetts; **Maria Kasparova**, Bergen Community College, New Jersey; **Gail Kellersberger**, University of Houston-Downtown, Texas; **Christina Kelso**, Austin Peay State University, Tennessee; **Daryl Kinney**, Los Angeles City College, California; **Leslie Kosel Eckstein**, Hillsborough Community College, Florida; **Beth Kozbial Ernst**, University of Wisconsin-Eau Claire, Wisconsin; **Jennifer Lacroix**, Center for English Language and Orientation Programs: Boston University, Massachusetts; **Stuart Landers**, Missouri State University, Missouri; **Margaret V. Layton**, University of Nevada, Reno Intensive English Language Center, Nevada; **Heidi Lieb**, Bergen Community College, New Jersey; **Kerry Linder**, Language Studies International New York, New York; **Jenifer Lucas-Uygun**, Passaic County Community College, New Jersey; **Alison MacAdams**, Approach International Student Center, Massachusetts; **Craig Machado**, Norwalk Community College, Connecticut; **Andrew J. MacNeill**, Southwestern College, California; **Melanie A. Majeski**, Naugatuck Valley Community College, Connecticut; **Wendy Maloney**, College of DuPage, Illinois; **Chris Mares**, University of Maine – Intensive English Institute, Maine; **Josefina Mark**, Union County College, New Jersey; **Connie Mathews**, Nashville State Community College, Tennessee; **Bette Matthews**, Mid-Pacific Institute, Hawaii; **Marla McDaniels Heath**, Norwalk Community College, Connecticut; **Kimberly McGrath Moreira**, University of Miami, Florida; **Sara McKinnon**, College of Marin, California; **Christine Mekkaoui**, Pittsburg State University, Kansas; **Holly A. Milkowart**, Johnson County Community College, Kansas; **Warren Mosher**, University of Miami, Florida; **Lukas Murphy**, Westchester Community College, New York; **Elena Nehrebecki**, Hudson Community College, New Jersey; **Bjarne Nielsen**, Central Piedmont Community College, North Carolina; **David Nippoldt**, Reedley College, California; **Lucia Parsley**, Virginia Commonwealth University, Virginia; **Wendy Patriquin**, Parkland College, Illinois; **Marion Piccolomini**, Communicate With Ease, LTD, Pennsylvania; **Carolyn Prager**, Spanish-American Institute, New York; **Eileen Prince**, Prince Language Associates Incorporated, Massachusetts; **Sema Pulak**, Texas A & M University, Texas; **James T. Raby**, Clark University, Massachusetts; **Anouchka Rachelson**, Miami-Dade College, Florida; **Lynn Ramage Schaefer**, University of Central Arkansas, Arkansas; **Sherry Rasmussen**, DePaul University, Illinois; **Amy Renehan**, University of Washington, Washington; **Esther Robbins**, Prince George's Community College, Pennsylvania; **Helen Roland**, Miami Dade College, Florida; **Linda Roth**, Vanderbilt University English Language Center, Tennessee; **Janine Rudnick**, El Paso Community College, Texas; **Rita Rutkowski Weber**, University of Wisconsin – Milwaukee, Wisconsin; **Elena Sapp**, INTO Oregon State University, Oregon; **Margaret Shippey**, Miami Dade College, Florida; **Lisa Sieg**, Murray State University, Kentucky; **Alison Stamps**, ESL Center at Mississippi State University, Mississippi; **Peggy Street**, ELS Language Centers, Miami, Florida; **Lydia Streiter**, York College Adult Learning Center, New York; **Nicholas Taggart**, Arkansas State University, Arkansas; **Marcia Takacs**, Coastline Community College, California; **Tamara Teffeteller**, University of California Los Angeles, American Language Center, California; **Rebecca Toner**, English Language Programs, University of Pennsylvania, Pennsylvania; **William G. Trudeau**, Missouri Southern State University, Missouri; **Troy Tucker**, Edison State College, Florida; **Maria Vargas-O'Neel**, Miami Dade College, Florida; **Amerca Vazquez**, Miami Dade College, Florida; **Alison Vinande**, Modesto Junior College, California; **Christie Ward**, Intensive English Language Program, Central Connecticut State University, Connecticut; **Colin S. Ward**, Lone Star College-North Harris, Texas; **Denise L. Warner**, Lansing Community College, Michigan; **Wendy Wish-Bogue**, Valencia Community College, Florida; **Cissy Wong**, Sacramento City College, California; **Kimberly Yoder**, Kent State University, ESL Center, Ohio.

ASIA **Teoh Swee Ai**, Universiti Teknologi Mara, Malaysia; **Nor Azni Abdullah**, Universiti Teknologi Mara, Malaysia; **Thomas E. Bieri**, Nagoya College, Japan; **Paul Dournhoncaque**, Seoul National University of Technology, Korea; **Michael C. Cheng**, National Chengchi University, Taiwan; **Fu-Dong Chiou**, National Taiwan University, Taiwan; **Derek Currie**, Korea University, Sejong Institute of Foreign Language Studies, Korea; **Christoph A. Hafner**, City University of Hong Kong, Hong Kong; **Wenhua Hsu**, I-Shou University, Taiwan; **Helen Huntley**, Hanoi University, Vietnam; **Rob Higgens**, Ritsumeikan University, Japan; **Shih Fan Kao**, JinWen University of Science and Technology, Taiwan; **Ikuko Kashiwabara**, Osaka Electro-Communication University, Japan; **Richard S. Lavin**, Prefectural University of Kumamoto, Japan; **Mike Lay**, American Institute, Cambodia; **Byoung-Kyo Lee**, Yonsei University, Korea; **Lin Li**, Capital Normal University, China; **Hudson Murrell**, Baiko Gakuin University, Japan; **Keiichi Narita**, Hirosaki University, Japan; **Huynh Thi Ai Nguyen**, Vietnam USA Society, Vietnam; **James Pham**, IDP Phnom Penh, Cambodia; **Duncan Rose**, British Council, Singapore; **Simone Samuels**, The Indonesia Australia Language Foundation Jakarta, Indonesia; **Wang Songmei**, Beijing Institute of Education Faculty, China; **Chien-Wen Jenny Tseng**, National Sun Yat-Sen University, Taiwan; **Hajime Uematsu**, Hirosaki University, Japan

AUSTRALIA **Susan Austin**, University of South Australia, **Joanne Cummins**, Swinburne College; **Pamela Humphreys**, Griffith University

LATIN AMERICA AND THE CARIBBEAN **Ramon Aguilar**, Universidad Tecnológica de Hermosillo, México; **Livia de Araujo Donnini Rodrigues**, University of São Paolo, Brazil; **Cecilia Avila**, Universidad de Xapala, México; Beth Bartlett, Centro Cultural Colombo Americano, Cali, Colombia; **Raúl Billini**, Colegio Loyola, Dominican Republic; **Nohora Edith Bryan**, Universidad de La Sabana, Colombia; **Raquel Hernández Cantú**, Instituto Tecnológico de Monterrey, Mexico; **Millie Commander**, Inter American University of Puerto Rico, Puerto Rico; **Edwin Marín-Arroyo**, Instituto Tecnológico de Costa Rica; **Rosario Mena**, Instituto Cultural Dominico-Americano, Dominican Republic; **Elizabeth Ortiz Lozada**, COPEI-COPOL English Institute, Ecuador; **Gilberto Rios Zamora**, Sinaloa State Language Center, Mexico; **Patricia Veciños**, El Instituto Cultural Argentino Norteamericano, Argentina

MIDDLE EAST AND NORTH AFRICA **Tom Farkas**, American University of Cairo, Egypt; **Ghada Hozayen**, Arab Academy for Science, Technology and Maritime Transport, Egypt; **Barbara R. Reimer**, CERTESL, UAE University; **Jodi Lefort**, Sultan Qaboos University

Dedicated to Kristin L. Johannsen, whose love for the world's cultures and concern for the world's environment were an inspiration to family, friends, students, and colleagues.

Scope and Sequence

Unit	Academic Pathways	Vocabulary	Listening Skills
1 **Gender and Society** *Page 1* **Academic Track:** Interdisciplinary	**Lesson A:** Listening to a Lecture Giving a Presentation about a Name **Lesson B:** Listening to a Conversation between Classmates Participating in a Mini-Debate	Understanding meaning from context Using new vocabulary in a survey Using new vocabulary to give reasons	Note-taking Listening for main ideas Listening for details **Pronunciation:** *Can/can't*
2 **Reproducing Life** *Page 21* **Academic Track:** Life Science	**Lesson A:** Listening to a Conversation about a Documentary Discussing Species Conservation **Lesson B:** Listening to a Conversation between Classmates Creating and Presenting a Group Plan	Understanding meaning from context Using new vocabulary to complete an article Understanding suffixes Using a dictionary to learn new words	Listening for main ideas Listening for details **Pronunciation:** Stress patterns before suffixes Emphasis on key words
3 **Human Migration** *Page 41* **Academic Track:** Sociology	**Lesson A:** Listening to a PowerPoint® Lecture Discussing Case Studies **Lesson B:** Listening to a Small Group Discussion Giving a Group Presentation	Understanding meaning from context Using a dictionary	Predicting content Listening for main ideas Listening for details **Pronunciation:** Fast speech
4 **Fascinating Planet** *Page 61* **Academic Track:** Earth Science	**Lesson A:** Listening to a Documentary Explaining Causes and Effects **Lesson B:** Listening to an Informal Conversation Doing and Discussing Internet Research	Using context clues Choosing the correct word	Tuning out distractions Taking notes on a documentary **Pronunciation:** Intonation for choices and lists
5 **Making a Living, Making a Difference** *Page 81* **Academic Track:** Economics/Business **Independent Student Handbook** *Page 201*	**Lesson A:** Listening to a Guest Speaker Making Comparisons **Lesson B:** Listening to a Class Question and Answer Session Giving a Presentation Based on Internet Research	Understanding meaning from context Using new vocabulary in a conversation	Understanding a speaker's purpose Taking notes on a lecture **Pronunciation:** Contractions

Grammar	Speaking Skills	Viewing	Critical Thinking Skills
Indefinite pronouns Indefinite pronouns and pronoun usage	Talking about rules and expectations Using inclusive language Talking about rules and expectations in the past **Student-to-Student:** Greeting a friend after a long time **Presentation Skill:** Preparing notes for speaking	**Video:** *Wodaabe* Note-taking while viewing Viewing for details	Interpreting information from a map Expressing and explaining opinions Relating information to personal experience Using a graphic organizer Arguing an opinion using reasons **Critical Thinking Focus:** Evaluating reasons
Adjective clauses Making suggestions	Explaining a process Making suggestions **Student-to-Student:** Asking for repetition **Presentation Skill:** Using specific details	**Video:** *Turtle Excluder* Understanding main ideas Taking notes while viewing	Identifying information Using new vocabulary in a discussion Organizing ideas for a presentation Analyzing information for relevance Preparing a research study **Critical Thinking Focus:** Judging the relevance of information
Adjectives with *enough, not enough,* and *too* Using the past continuous tense	Asking for reasons Telling a personal history **Student-to-Student:** Asking sensitive questions **Presentation Skill:** Using visuals	**Video:** *Turkish Germany* Viewing for general concepts Viewing for specific information	Interpreting information on a map Understanding visuals (a line graph) Applying new grammar in discussions Proposing solutions to a problem Assessing information **Critical Thinking Focus:** Analyzing information
The simple past with past continuous tense So + adjective + *that*	Talking about historical events Talking about causes and effects Responding to suggestions **Student-to-Student:** Responding to suggestions **Presentation Skill:** Making eye contact	**Video:** *The Giant's Causeway* Viewing for numbers Taking notes in a T-chart while viewing	Recognizing vocabulary words Practicing using words and phrases to indicate causes and effects Categorizing information using a T-chart Deducing meaning from context Synthesizing information from the unit **Critical Thinking Focus:** Using graphic organizers
Making comparisons with *as . . . as* Indirect questions	Using numbers and statistics Using indirect questions **Student-to-Student:** Showing interest in what a speaker is saying **Presentation Skill:** Practicing and timing your presentation	**Video:** *The Business of Cranberries* Viewing for general concepts Viewing for specific information	Interpreting information from a chart Demonstrating comprehension of information from a listening Planning a presentation Formulating sentences based on visuals Evaluating different charity organizations **Critical Thinking Focus:** Identifying the speaker's purpose

EXPLORE A UNIT   THE PATHWAY TO ACADEMIC SUCCESS...

Each unit consists of two lessons which include the following sections:

- Building Vocabulary
- Using Vocabulary
- Developing Listening Skills
- Exploring Spoken English
- Speaking (called "Engage" in Lesson B)

- An **academic pathway** is clearly labeled for learners, starting with formal listening (e.g., lectures) and moving to a more informal context (e.g., a conversation between students in a study group).

- The **"Exploring the Theme"** section provides a visual introduction to the unit and encourages learners to think critically and share ideas about the unit topic.

THE PATHWAY TO ACADEMIC SUCCESS...

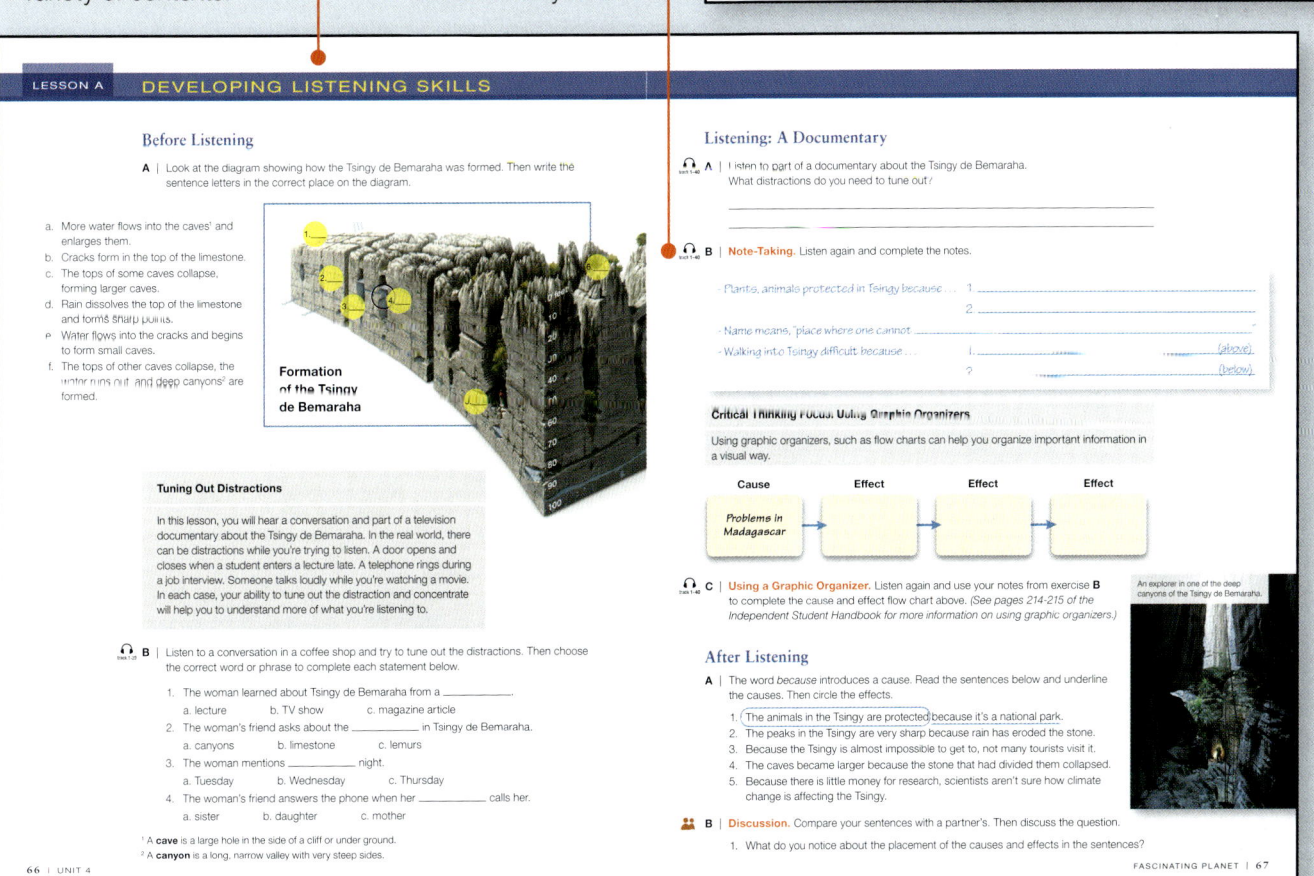

Key academic and high-frequency vocabulary is introduced, practiced, and expanded throughout each unit. Lessons A and B each present and practice 10 terms.

Critical thinking activities are integrated in every unit encouraging continuous engagement in developing academic skills.

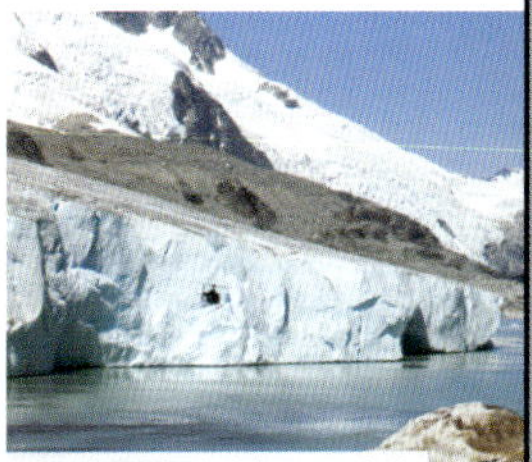

A **"Developing Listening Skills"** section follows a before, during, and after approach to give learners the tools necessary to master listening skills for a variety of contexts.

Note-taking activities encourage learners to listen for and consolidate key information, reinforcing the language, and allowing learners to think critically about the information they hear.

USING VOCABULARY

D | **Discussion.** Work with a partner. Discuss the questions.

1. Do you think Jiuzhaigou will stay clean and beautiful with 2 million tourists visiting every year? Why, or why not?
2. What do you think park officials could do to keep the park clean and beautiful?

track 1-38 **E** | **Meaning from Context.** Read about glaciers and circle the correct word choice. Then listen and check your answers.

The lakes in Jiuzhaigou National Park were (formed/dissolved) by glaciers—huge bodies of ice. Today there are glaciers high up in some mountains, but at other times in the earth's history colder temperatures allowed glaciers to exist in much larger areas.

As glaciers grow and move, they push dirt and (stone/rare) along with them. This material, along with the ice itself, is (lack/sharp) enough to (erode/protect) the land where the glaciers move. In this way, hills can become flat land, and flat land can become holes. Later, when temperatures become warmer and the glaciers melt, lakes are the result.

Glacial ice can become water in another way, too. At the bottom edge of a glacier, (cracks/forms) can develop and large pieces of ice can fall into the water below. These pieces of ice then melt and become part of the body of water.

In British Columbia, Canada, a helicopter approaches the bottom edge of a glacier and the lake that it has formed.

F | **Discussion.** Work with a partner. Discuss the questions.

1. How is climate change affecting the world's glaciers?
2. How do changes to glaciers affect the world in general?

G | **Critical Thinking.** Form a group with two or three other students and discuss the questions.

1. National parks are rare in some countries and common in others. Which is true in your country?
2. Jiuzhaigou has no lack of tourists. What do you think is the greater benefit of this tourism: the money spent by tourists, or the love and respect for nature tourists feel when they visit the park?
3. The beautiful mountains and lakes in Jiuzhaigou took millions of years to form. How long do you think it would take for human beings to have a major effect on them?
4. Worldwide, there is a limited amount of money and resources for the protection of rare animals such as panda bears. How should people decide which species are worth protecting?

FASCINATING PLANET | 65

LESSON A

DEVELOPING LISTENING SKILLS

Before Listening

A | Look at the diagram showing how the Tsingy de Bemaraha was formed. Then write the sentence letters in the correct place on the diagram.

a. More water flows into the caves[1] and enlarges them.
b. Cracks form in the top of the limestone.
c. The tops of some caves collapse, forming larger caves.
d. Rain dissolves the top of the limestone and forms sharp points.
e. Water flows into the cracks and begins to form small caves.
f. The tops of other caves collapse, the water runs out, and deep canyons[2] are formed.

Tuning Out Distractions

In this lesson, you will hear a conversation and part of a television documentary about the Tsingy de Bemaraha. In the real world, there can be distractions while you're trying to listen. A door opens and closes when a student enters a lecture late. A telephone rings during a job interview. Someone talks loudly while you're watching a movie. In each case, your ability to tune out the distraction and concentrate will help you to understand more of what you're listening to.

track 1-39 **B** | Listen to a conversation in a coffee shop and try to tune out the distractions. Then choose the correct word or phrase to complete each statement below.

1. The woman learned about Tsingy de Bemaraha from a __________.
   a. lecture   b. TV show   c. magazine article
2. The woman's friend asks about the __________ in Tsingy de Bemaraha.
   a. canyons   b. limestone   c. lemurs
3. The woman mentions __________ night.
   a. Tuesday   b. Wednesday   c. Thursday
4. The woman's friend answers the phone when her __________ calls her.
   a. sister   b. daughter   c. mother

[1] A **cave** is a large hole in the side of a cliff or under ground.
[2] A **canyon** is a long, narrow valley with very steep sides.

66 | UNIT 4

Listening: A Documentary

track 1-40 **A** | Listen to part of a documentary about the Tsingy de Bemaraha. What distractions do you need to tune out?

____

____

track 1-40 **B** | **Note-Taking.** Listen again and complete the notes.

- Plants, animals protected in Tsingy because ... 1. __________
  2. __________
- Name means, "place where one cannot __________"
- Walking into Tsingy difficult because ... 1. __________ (above)
  2. __________ (below)

Critical Thinking Focus: Using Graphic Organizers

Using graphic organizers, such as flow charts can help you organize important information in a visual way.

Cause	Effect	Effect	Effect
Problems in Madagascar →	→	→	

track 1-40 **C** | **Using a Graphic Organizer.** Listen again and use your notes from exercise **B** to complete the cause and effect flow chart above. *(See pages 214-215 of the Independent Student Handbook for more information on using graphic organizers.)*

An explorer in one of the deep canyons of the Tsingy de Bemaraha.

After Listening

A | The word *because* introduces a cause. Read the sentences below and underline the causes. Then circle the effects.

1. The animals in the Tsingy are protected because it's a national park.
2. The peaks in the Tsingy are very sharp because rain has eroded the stone.
3. Because the Tsingy is almost impossible to get to, not many tourists visit it.
4. The caves became larger because the stone that had divided them collapsed.
5. Because there is little money for research, scientists aren't sure how climate change is affecting the Tsingy.

B | **Discussion.** Compare your sentences with a partner's. Then discuss the question.

1. What do you notice about the placement of the causes and effects in the sentences?

FASCINATING PLANET | 67

THE PATHWAY TO ACADEMIC SUCCESS...

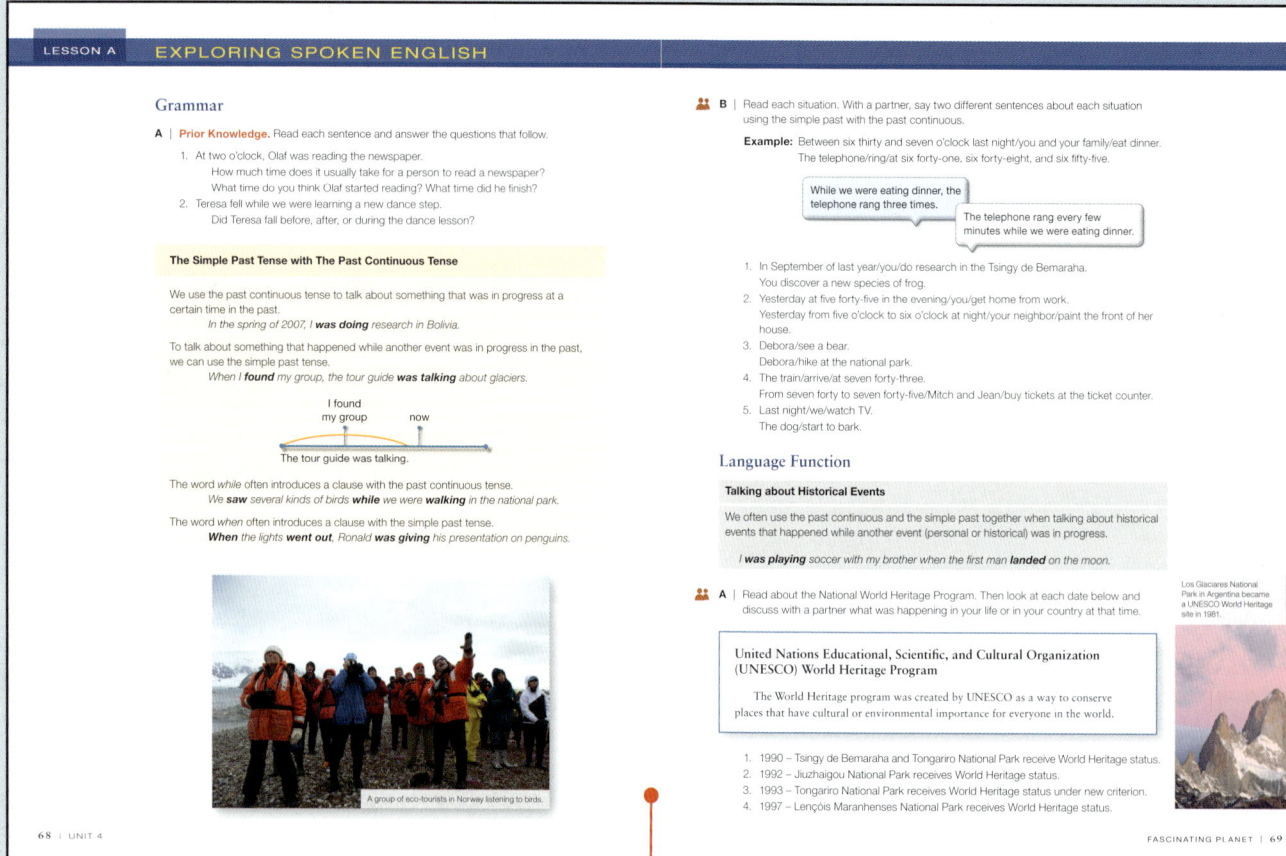

- The **"Exploring Spoken English"** section allows students to examine and practice specific grammar points and language functions from the unit while enabling them to sharpen their listening and speaking skills.

- Lesson A closes with a **full page of "Speaking" activities** including pair and group work activities, increasing learner confidence when communicating in English.

- **A variety of activity types** simulate the academic classroom where multiple skills must be applied simultaneously for success.

THE PATHWAY TO ACADEMIC SUCCESS...

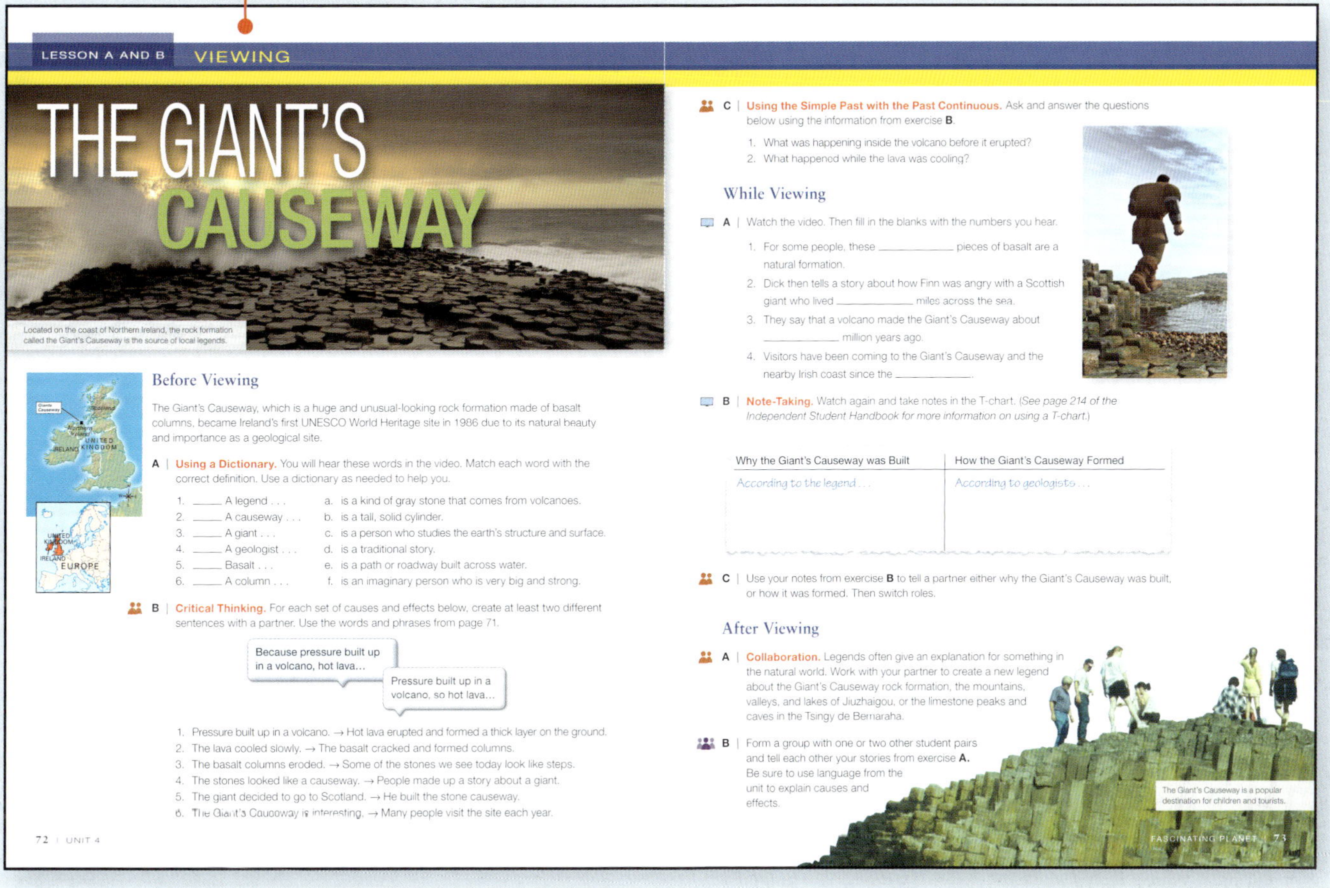

A **"Viewing" section** works as a content-bridge between Lesson A and Lesson B and includes two pages of activities based on a fascinating video from National Geographic Digital Media.

● **A DVD for each level** contains 10 authentic videos from National Geographic Digital Media specially adapted for English language learners.

EXPLORE A UNIT

THE PATHWAY TO ACADEMIC SUCCESS...

• **"Presentation Skills" boxes** offer helpful tips and suggestions for successful academic presentations.

• An **"Engage" section** challenges learners with an end-of-unit presentation project. Speaking tips are offered for formal and informal group communication, instructing students to interact appropriately in different academic situations.

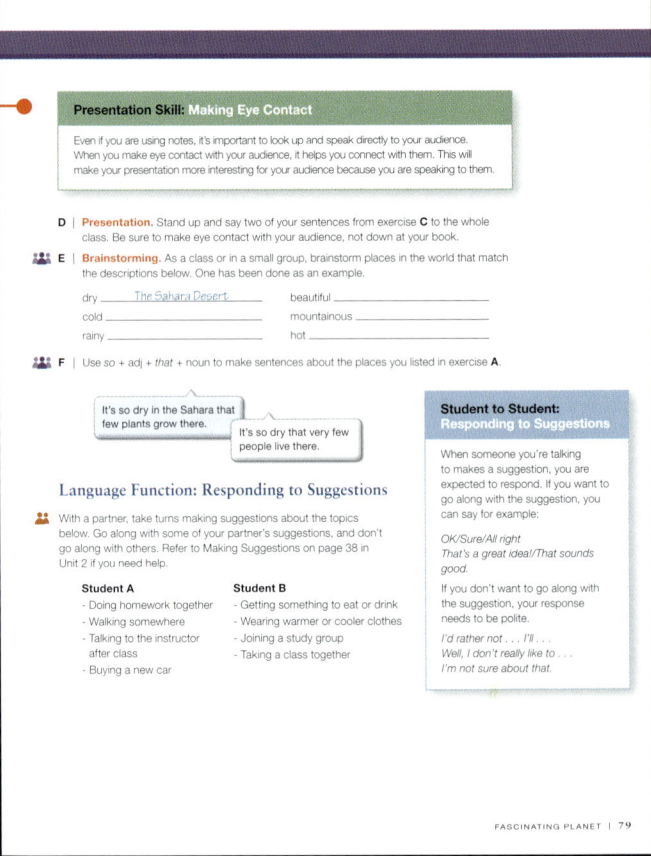

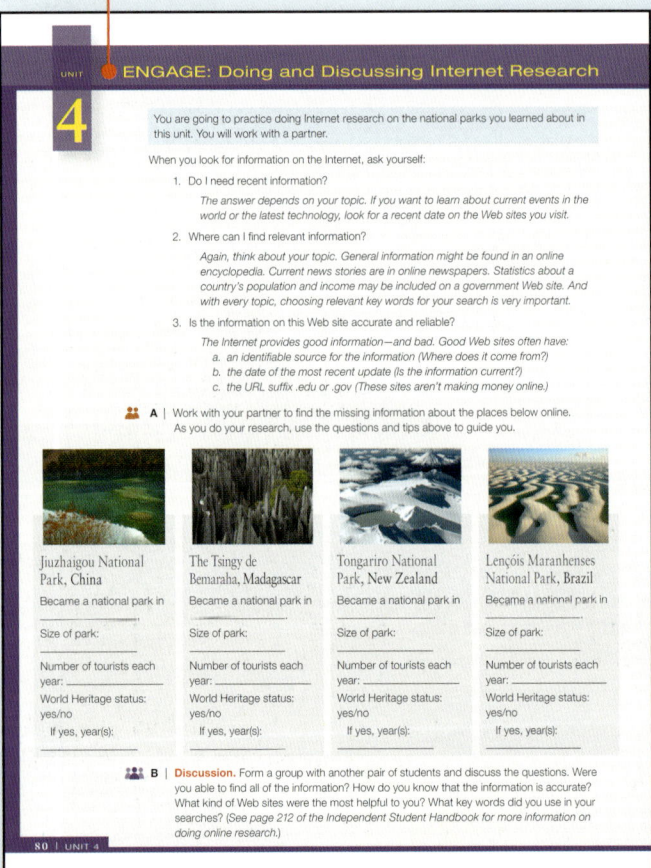

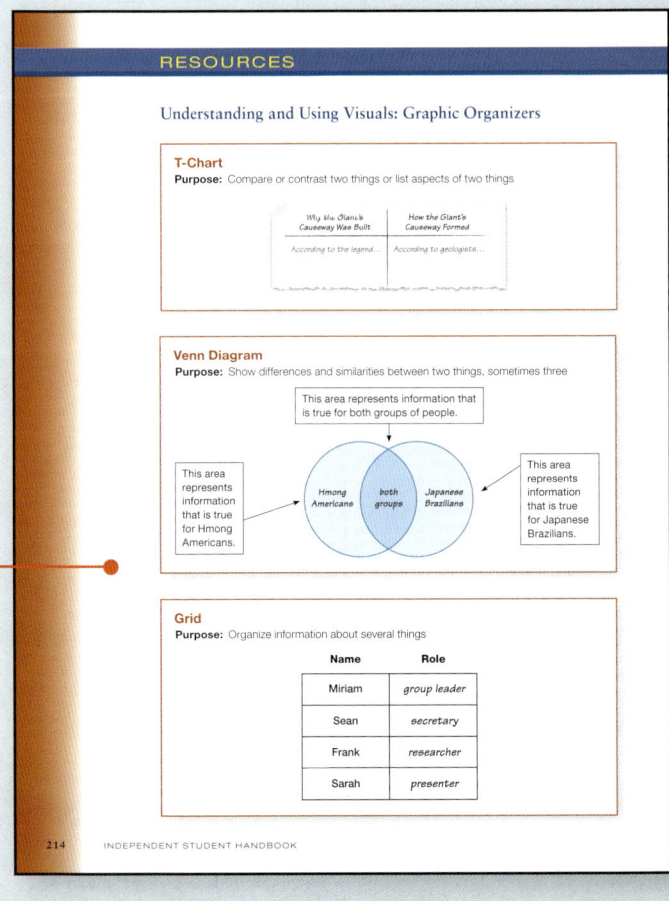

• A 19-page **"Independent Student Handbook"** is conveniently located in the back of the book and provides helpful self-study strategies for students to become better independent learners.

EXPLORE A UNIT

STUDENT AND INSTRUCTOR RESOURCES (for each level)

For the Teacher:

A **Teacher's Guide** is available in an easy-to-use format and includes teacher's notes, expansion activities, and answer keys for activities in the student book.

Perfect for integrating language practice with exciting visuals, **video clips from National Geographic Digital Media** bring the sights and sounds of our world into the classroom.

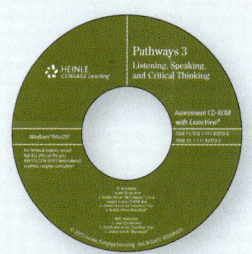

The Assessment CD-ROM with ExamView® is a test generating software program with a data bank of ready-made questions designed to allow teachers to assess students quickly and effectively.

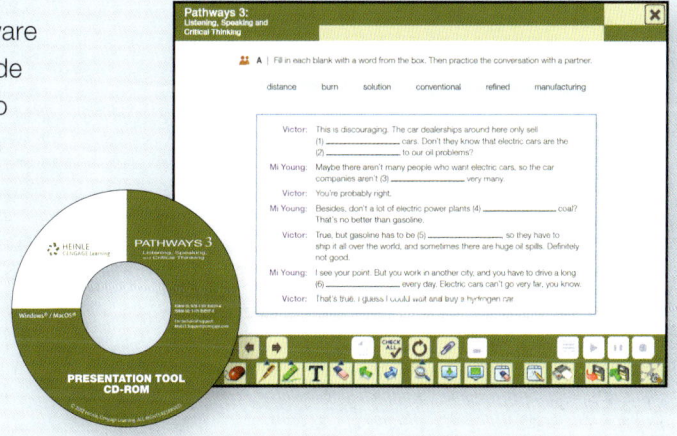

Bringing a new dimension to the language learning classroom, the **Classroom Presentation Tool CD-ROM** makes instruction clearer and learning easier through interactive activities, audio and video clips, and Presentation Worksheets.

For the Student:

The **Student Book** helps students achieve academic success in and outside of the classroom.

Audio CDs contain the audio recordings for the exercises in the student books.

Powered by MyELT, the **Online Workbook** has both teacher-led and self-study options. It contains 10 National Geographic video clips, supported by interactive, automatically graded activities that practice the skills learned in the student books.

Visit elt.heinle.com/pathways for additional teacher and student resources.

CREDITS

LISTENING AND TEXT

7: Adapted from, "The King Herself", by Chip Brown: National Geographic Magazine, April 2009, **25:** Adapted from "Every Bird a King", by Tom O'Neill: National Geographic Magazine, September 2009, **34:** Adapted from "Love & Lies (Orchids)", by Michael Pollan: National Geographic Magazine, September 2009, **29:** Adapted from "Recipe for a Resurrection", by Tom Mueller: National Geographic Magazine, May 2009, **29:** Adapted from "Ox Redux", by Juli Berwald: National Geographic Magazine, July 2010, Conservation Feature, **46–47:** Adapted from "The Emptied Prairie", by Charles Bowden: National Geographic Magazine, January 2008, **64–65:** Adapted from "To Paradise, by the Busload: Jiuzhaigou", by Edward Hoagland: National Georgrapic Magazine, March 2009, **69:** Adapted from "Living on a Razor's Edge", by Neil Shea: National Geographic Magazine, November 2009, **74:** Adapted from, "Between Fire and Ice", by Mel White: National Geographic Magazine, July 2009, **76:** Adapted from, "A Sea of Dunes", by Ronaldo Ribeiro: National Geographic Magazine, July 2010, **86:** Adapted from "India Snake Hunters find Antidote to Joblessness", by Pallava Bagla: National Geographic News, February 2003, **89:** Adapted from "Kudzu Entrepreneurs find Gold in Green Menace", by John Roach: National Geographic News, April 2005.

PHOTOS

Cover: Terry W. Eggers/CORBIS, **2:** Jimmy Chinn/National Geographic Image Collection, **2:** Cary Wolinsky/National Geographic Image Collection, **3:** Ivan Kashinsky/National Geographic Image Collection, **3:** Randy Olson/National Geographic Image Collection, **3:** AP Photo/Tomas Munita, **3:** Jodi Cobb/National Geographic Image Collection, **3:** Ed Kashi / National Geographic Image Collection, **4:** Pierre Perrin/Sygma/Corbis **4:** Dulwich Picture Gallery, London, UK/The Bridgeman Art Library International, **4:** Moviestore collection Ltd/Alamy, **6:** Kenneth Garrett/National Geographic Image Collection, **8:** Winfield Parks/National Geographic Image Collection, **11:** ColorBlind Images/conica/Getty Images, **12:** Carol Beckwith/National Geographic Image Collection, **13:** Karen Kasmauski/National Geographic Image Collection, **13:** Robert Estall photo agency/Alamy, **14:** Tyrone Turner, **14:** Todd Gipstein/National Geographic Image Collection, **15:** Vstock LLC/Tetra images/Jupiter Images, **16:** GWImages, 2010/Shutterstock.com, **16:** Sean Locke/istockphoto.com, **19:** Monkey Business Images/Shutterstock.com, **20:** Losevsky Pavel/Shutterstock.com, **21:** Matthias Breiter/Minden Pictures, **22–23:** Unterthiner, Stefano/National Geographic Image Collection, **23:** Tom Vezo/Minden Pictures/National Geographic Image Collection, **23:** George Grall/National Geographic Image Collection, **23:** Darlyne A. Murawski/National Geographic Image Collection, **24:** John Eastcott and Yva Momatiuk/National Geographic Image Collection, **24:** John Eastcott and Yva Momatiuk/National Geographic Image Collection, **24:** Yva Momatiuk and John Eastcott/Minden Pictures, **24:** Unterthiner, Stefano/National Geographic Image Collection, **25:** Unterthiner, Stefano/National Geographic Image Collection, **26:** Unterthiner, Stefano/National Geographic Image Collection, **27:** Mauricio Handler/National Geographic Image Collection, **27:** Gail Johnson/Shutterstock.com, **28:** Karen Kasmauski/National Geographic Image Collection, **28:** Aristide Economopoulos/Star Ledger/Corbis, **29:** Tim Laman/National Geographic Image Collection, **30:** David Fleetham/Visuals Unlimited, Inc/Visuals Unlimited/Getty Images, **31:** Peter ten Broecke/istockphoto.com, **32:** George Grall/National Geographic/Getty Images, **33:** Robert Sisson/National Geographic Image Collection, **33:** Norbert Wu/ Minden Pictures/National Geographic Image Collection, **34:** Christian Ziegler, **34:** Christian Ziegler/National Geographic Image Collection, **36:** Jonathan Blair/National Geographic Image Collection, **37:** Christian Ziegler/National Geographic Image Collection, **38:** Monkey Business Images/Shutterstock.com, **39:** Dean Bertoncelj/Shutterstock.com, **41:** Theo Westenberger/National Geographic Image Collection, **42:** National Geographic Image Collection, **43:** Reza/National Geographic Image Collection, **43:** Carsten Koall/Visum/The Image Works, **43:** Howell Walker/National Geographic Image Collection, **45:** PANOS PICTURES/National Geographic Image Collection, **46:** Eugene Richards/National Geographic Image Collection, **46:** Andre Jenny/Alamy, **47:** Courtesy of Andrew Filer, **47:** Alaska Stock Images/National Geographic Image Collection, **47:** Eugene Richards/National Geographic Image Collection, **48:** Radu Razvan/Shutterstock.com, **49:** Orange Line Media/Shutterstock.com, **51:** J. Baylor Roberts/National Geographic Image Collection, **51:** Jupiterimages, **51:** Richard Mulonga/ Newscom, **52:** Sean Gallup/Getty Images, **53:** Cotton Coulson/National Geographic Image Collection, **53:** turkishblue, 2010/Shutterstock.com, **55:** Steve Skjold/Alamy, **55:** David Davis Photoproductions/Alamy, **56:** Maggie Steber/National Geographic Image Collection, **56:** Michael Nichols/National Geographic Image Collection, **59:** Chuck Pefley/Alamy, **60:** The Library of Congress, **60:** Chris Johns/National Geographic Image Collection, **60:** t14/ZUMA Press/Newscom, **61:** Dai Rui/National Geographic Image Collection, **62–63:** Stephen Alvarez/National Geographic Image Collection, **63:** Stephen Alvarez/National Geographic Image Collection, **63:** Stephen Alvarez/National Geographic Image Collection, **64:** Michael S. Yamashita/National Geographic Image Collection, **65:** Taylor S. Kennedy/National Geographic Image Collection, **67:** Stephen Alvarez/National Geographic Image Collection, **68:** KEENPRESS/National Geographic Image Collection, **69:** John Eastcott and Yva Momatiuk/National Geographic Image Collection, **72:** Jim Richardson/National Geographic Image Collection, **73:** Kuttig-Travel/Alamy, **73:** Mark Snyder/American Artists Rep., Inc., **74:** Stuart Franklin/National Geographic Image Collection, **75:** Stuart Franklin/National Geographic Image Collection, **76:** George Steinmetz/National Geographic Image Collection, **77:** George Steinmetz/National Geographic Image Collection, **78:** Paul Nicklen/National Geographic Image Collection, **80:** Michael S. Yamashita/National Geographic Image Collection, **80:** George Steinmetz/National Geographic Image Collection, **80:** Stephen Alvarez/National Geographic Image Collection, **80:** George Steinmetz/National Geographic Image Collection, **81:** NATIONAL GEOGRAPHIC/MY SHOT/National Geographic Image Collection, **81:** NATIONAL GEOGRAPHIC/MY SHOT/National Geographic Image Collection, **82–83:** Chris Rainier/National Geographic Image Collection, **83:** Pete Ryan/National Geographic Image Collection, **83:** Justin Guariglia/National Geographic Image Collection, **84:** Volkmar K. Wentzel/National Geographic Image Collection, **85:** Aaron Huey/National Geographic Image Collection, **86:** Michael & Patricia Fogden/Minden Pictures/Getty Images, **87:** James P. Blair/National Geographic Image Collection, **88:** Melissa Farlow/National Geographic Image Collection, **89:** AP Photo/Mary Ann Chastain, **91:** Chris Hill/National Geographic Image Collection, **91:** Justin Guarigila/National Geographic Image Collection, **91:** Aaron Huey/National Geographic Image Collection, **91:** Michael & Patricia Fogden/Minden Pictures/Getty Images, **91:** AP Photo/Mary Ann Chastain, **92:** Rich Reid/National Geographic Image Collection, **92:** Chris Johns/National Geographic Image Collection, **93:** Bill Curtsinger/National Geographic Image Collection, **93:** Sean Sherstone/iStockphoto.com, **95:** Jonas Bendiksen/National Geographic Image Collection, **96:** Annie Griffiths/National Geographic Image Collection, **97:** Roger Leo/PhotoLibrary, **99:** Noah Seelam/AFP/Getty Images, **99:** Amy White & Al Petteway/National Geographic Image Collection, **99:** Michael Melford/National Geographic Image Collection, **99:** Shehzad Noorani/PhotoLibrary, **100:** James P. Blair/National Geographic Image Collection, **100:** Per-Anders Pettersson/Getty Images News/Getty Images, **100:** Maria Stenzel/National Geographic Image Collection.

continued on p.224

Gender and Society

UNIT 1

ACADEMIC PATHWAYS
Lesson A: Listening to a Lecture
Giving a Presentation about a Name
Lesson B: Listening to a Conversation between Classmates
Participating in a Mini-Debate

Think and Discuss

1. What are these people doing?
2. What surprises you about this picture?
3. Would you enjoy watching this sports event? Explain.

A Sunday sports event in El Alto, Bolivia

Exploring the Theme: Gender and Society

A | Look at the photos and read the captions. Then discuss the questions.

1. Do you think any of the activities shown should be for men or women only? Explain.
2. Do you think gender (being male or female) is something we are born with or learn? Explain.

B | Look at the map. Then discuss the questions.

1. The map shows popular names for men and women in different countries. (The women's names are listed first.) According to the map, what is a popular woman's name in Brazil? What's a popular man's name in Japan?
2. What are some popular names for men and women in your country?

A woman climbs up rock and ice in British Columbia, **Canada**.

A woman works at a steel factory in Pennsylvania, **USA**.

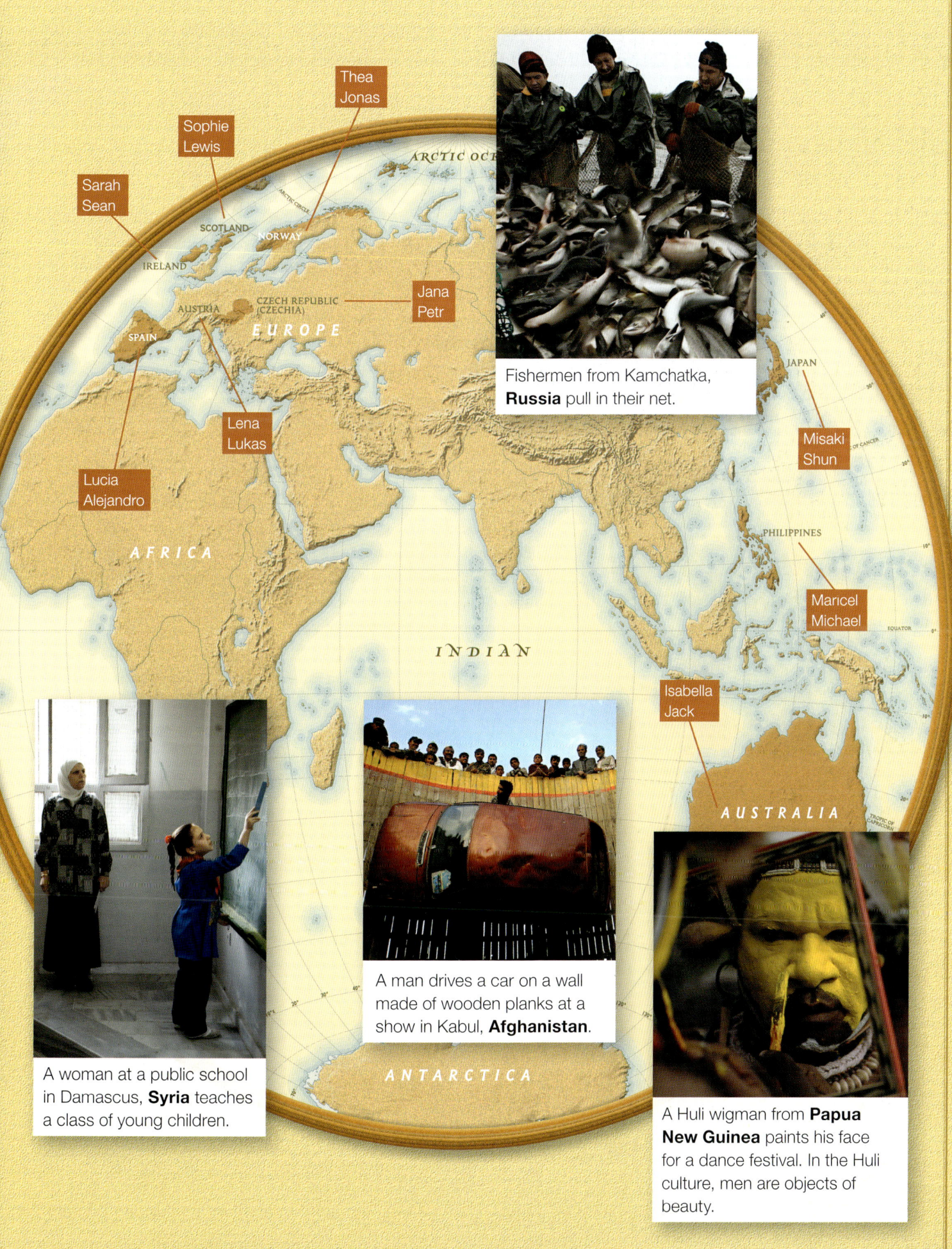

Fishermen from Kamchatka, **Russia** pull in their net.

A woman at a public school in Damascus, **Syria** teaches a class of young children.

A man drives a car on a wall made of wooden planks at a show in Kabul, **Afghanistan**.

A Huli wigman from **Papua New Guinea** paints his face for a dance festival. In the Huli culture, men are objects of beauty.

LESSON A | BUILDING VOCABULARY

 A | **Meaning from Context.** Read and listen to the information. Notice the words in **blue**. These are words you will hear and use in Lesson A.

Kabuki is a traditional form of singing and dancing theater that is still popular in Japan. One unusual **characteristic** of *kabuki* is that all the **roles** of women are played by **male** actors called *onnagata*. These actors spend many years studying women's **behavior** and activities, such as sewing. Some people say that the actors are more **feminine** than real women are!

There are many examples of male actors who play roles of the opposite **gender**, but the **reverse** doesn't happen very often. *The Year of Living Dangerously* is a famous movie from the 1980s. It's about an Australian journalist who meets a news photographer during a time of terrible violence. Many people didn't notice that the star who played the role of Billy Kwan, the photographer, was actually a woman. Linda Hunt won an Academy Award for her acting in the movie. She gave Billy Kwan many characteristics that people think are **masculine**, especially courage.

In the time of William Shakespeare, women were **generally** not allowed to appear on a theater stage. In Shakespeare's plays, **female** characters like Juliet (in *Romeo and Juliet*) were played by young boys. Some of them became very famous, like Nathan Field in this picture. When their voices changed and they grew older, these actors had to start playing men's roles.

USING VOCABULARY

B | Complete each sentence with a word from the box. Use each word only once.

gender   behavior   characteristic   reverse   generally
role   male   female   masculine   feminine

1. _____, names that end in –y are girls' names, but there are exceptions, like *Jeffrey*.
2. In her new movie, Marisa Chang plays the _____ of a spy.
3. My dog's _____ is terrible! He chews on my furniture and takes food off my plate.
4. Only _____ animals can have babies.
5. Patience is an important _____ of a good teacher.
6. Little boys and girls learn a lot about _____ when they start school. They learn the things that boys and girls are supposed to do.
7. In the United States, women wear light colors like pink because they think they look more _____.
8. Usually more men than women are doctors, but in Russia, it's the _____. They have more female doctors there.
9. Some men grow beards because they think it makes them look more _____.
10. All the presidents of my country have been _____, except for our current leader. She was elected in 2010.

C | Read the statements and circle your opinions.

1. **Male** actors can play women's **roles** better than the reverse.	Agree	Not Sure	Disagree
2. If I were an actor/actress, I think I could play a **role** of the opposite **gender**.	Agree	Not Sure	Disagree
3. Children learn a lot of their **behavior** from watching TV.	Agree	Not Sure	Disagree
4. Playing with dolls won't make a little boy **feminine**.	Agree	Not Sure	Disagree
5. Some sports are too **masculine** for women to play.	Agree	Not Sure	Disagree
6. It's important for children to have both **male** and **female** teachers.	Agree	Not Sure	Disagree
7. Girls are **generally** better at math than boys are.	Agree	Not Sure	Disagree
8. Ideas about **gender** have changed in my country.	Agree	Not Sure	Disagree

D | **Discussion.** Compare your answers from the survey with your group. Give reasons and explanations for your opinions.

E | Tell the class about any statements that your group members all had the same opinion about.

LESSON A: DEVELOPING LISTENING SKILLS

Note-Taking

People generally speak more quickly than they write. To take good notes quickly while listening to a lecture, write only the most important ideas.

- Write only the key words.
  all kabuki actors men
- Don't write complete sentences.
  ~~In the~~ time of ~~William~~ Shakespeare, women ~~were generally~~ not allowed ~~to appear~~ on ~~theater~~ stage
- Use abbreviations (short forms) and symbols when possible.
  info information   *dr* doctor   *w/* with   → about

Hatshepsut wearing the traditionally male symbols of a lion's mane and a pharaoh's beard.

A | Cross out the unimportant words in these sentences using the advice from the chart above.

1. In some cultures men and women are expected to follow very strict rules about gender roles.
2. Children learn about gender roles when they watch the behavior of the people around them.

B | Think of abbreviations or symbols to replace these words and phrases.

1. year _____
2. without _____
3. less than _____
4. more than _____

(See pages 206-207 in the Independent Student Handbook for more information on note-taking.)

Before Listening

A | **Prior Knowledge.** Discuss the questions below with a partner.

1. Look at the picture. Who do you think this person was?
2. Do you think it's common or uncommon for a country to have a female president (prime minister, king, etc.)? Which countries can you think of whose leaders are women?

Listening: A Lecture

 A | **Listening for Main Ideas.** Listen to part of a lecture and read the notes below. Cross out the unimportant words and use symbols and abbreviations if possible.

1. gender socialization ~~is the way~~=how children learn ~~male and female~~ ♂/♀ gender roles
2. children learn their gender roles from their parents, their peers, schools, and their culture
3. parents give children different kinds of compliments; they compliment girls on their appearance, and they compliment boys on their actions.
4. peers make fun of children who are "different"; schools can have separate classes or school uniforms— pants for boys and skirts for girls; our culture also teaches us about gender roles

 B | Listen again and decide whether your notes in exercise **A** are brief, yet informative enough to help you remember the lecture.

C | **Listening for Details.** Listen to the next part of the talk and complete the notes.

- We ask: baby boy or girl? b/c later role in world depends on _____
  But:
1. gender roles today _____
2. some people don't _____
- In ancient Egypt, Hatshepsut became _____ (ca. 150 yrs. aft. Tut)
- While H ruled (_____ yrs.) constructed/repaired _____
  + _____ (wanted to be remembered)
- Early art: H w/ _____ characteristics. Later art:
  _____ (reason? maybe easier to keep power w/ ♂ looks)

After Listening

 Critical Thinking. Discuss the questions below with your group.

1. Which of the four ways children learn gender roles do you think is the most powerful? Why?
2. What do you remember about learning gender roles when you were a child?
3. Besides the reason given in the lecture, what are some other possible reasons why Hatshepsut's appearance in artwork changed over time?

LEGACY IN STONE
Hatshepsut erected many monuments along the Nile and in the Sinai but focused on her capital at Thebes, today the ruins of Karnak and Luxor.

LESSON A | EXPLORING SPOKEN ENGLISH

Language Function

Talking about Rules and Expectations

We use the following expressions to talk about rules.

Female students **must** wear dresses.	Taxi drivers **must not** overcharge the customers.
They **are required to** follow many other rules.	Sikhs **are forbidden to** cut their hair.
He **has to** arrive before the others.	They **aren't allowed to** become soldiers.

We use the following expressions to talk about expectations.

Women **are supposed to** take care of the children.	Women **aren't supposed to** complain.
Men **are expected to** play sports.	Men **aren't expected to** do housework.

These women are members of Bahrain's police force. They handle children's and women's cases.

A | Critical Thinking. Look at the picture. Match the columns to form the rules that you think these women must follow.

1. They are required ____
2. They have to ____
3. They are expected to stand up ____
4. They aren't allowed to ____
5. They are not supposed ____

a. when their officer walks in.
b. to wear jewelry.
c. handle men's cases.
d. to wear a uniform.
e. exercise everyday.

B | Compare your answers with a partner's. Then discuss the question below.

1. Which rules do you think would be the most difficult to follow? Why?
2. Do you think the male police officers have to follow the same rules? If not, how do you think the rules for men might be different?

C | **Using a Graphic Organizer.** Think about what the different rules and expectations are for boys and girls or men and women in your country. Make a T-chart in your notebook like the one below. (*See page 214 of the Independent Student Handbook for information on T-charts.*)

Boys/Men	Girls/Women
have to serve in the military for two years	are expected to take care of the children

 D | Use the notes in your T-chart to tell your partner about the different rules and expectations in your country. Take notes as you listen to your partner.

 E | Form a group with another pair of students. Talk about the most interesting information you learned from your partner.

Grammar

Indefinite Pronouns

Indefinite pronouns with *some-* *(someone, somebody, something, somewhere)* refer to an unspecified person, place, or thing.
  Most people marry **someone** who is close to their own age.

Indefinite pronouns with *every-* *(everyone, everybody, everything, everywhere)* refer to all of a group of people, places, or things.
  He has no clothes to wear. **Everything** in his closet is too small now.

Indefinite pronouns with *no-* *(no one, nobody, nothing, nowhere)* refer to none of a group of people, places, or things.
  Stella didn't go to the party because **nobody** told her about it.

We use indefinite pronouns with *any-* *(anyone, anybody, anything, anywhere)* when the person, place or thing is not important.
  You can choose the restaurant. **Anywhere** is fine with me.

We also use indefinite pronouns with *any-* in negative statements and in questions.
  We didn't go **anywhere** last night. Does **anybody** know what time it is?

Indefinite pronouns take the singular form of the verb.
  Everybody **likes** ice cream. Nothing **is** on the desk.

LESSON A

A | Read the sentences and circle the correct indefinite pronoun.

1. Kevin can't find his keys and he's looked (anywhere/(everywhere)/somewhere) for them.
2. I'm not really hungry. I don't want (something/nothing/anything) to eat right now.
3. This town is boring. There's (nothing/everything/anything) to do here at night.
4. I'm having a big party and I'm going to invite (nobody/everybody/anybody) in my class.
5. Has Aisha found (everyone/no one/anyone) who can teach her how to drive?

B | Read the sentences and circle the correct verb.

1. Everyone in the company (have/(has)/is) a specific role.
2. I think someone (are/is/has) at the door. I'll go downstairs and check.
3. (Does/Are/Is) anything bothering you? You look upset.
4. Everybody (is/are/seems) talking about the new movie. I really want to see it.
5. (Is/Does/Do) anybody interested in going hiking with me on Saturday?

C | Read the story below. Then discuss the questions with a partner.

Everybody, Somebody, Anybody, and Nobody

This is a little story about four people named Everybody, Somebody, Anybody, and Nobody. There was an important job to be done and Everybody was sure that Somebody would do it. Anybody could have done it, but Nobody did it. Somebody got angry about that because it was Everybody's job. Everybody thought that Anybody could do it, but Nobody realized that Everybody wouldn't do it. It ended up that Everybody blamed Somebody when Nobody did what Anybody could have done.

1. Do you think the story is funny? Why, or why not?
2. Have you ever experienced a similar situation? Explain.
3. Why do you think the author chose to use indefinite pronouns in this story?

D | Now read the information below. Then with a partner discuss situations when you think you should use *they* and *their* as indefinite pronouns.

Indefinite Pronouns and Pronoun Usage

Because indefinite pronouns are singular, they should be followed by singular pronouns. However, in casual speech, it's very common to use *they* or *their*. Using *they* and *their* also helps make language inclusive and non-sexist by not leaving out men or women. Using inclusive language is expected in formal academic and business situations.

Somebody left his phone on the chair. (formal usage, but not inclusive, excludes women)
Somebody left his or her phone on the chair. (formal usage, inclusive)
Somebody left their phone on the chair. (informal usage, inclusive)

SPEAKING

Giving a Presentation about a Name

A | Discussion. Work with a partner. Discuss the questions. Take notes on your partner's answers.

1. When you were a baby, who chose your name? Do you know why they chose that name?
2. Is your name common or uncommon?
3. Were you named after a relative?
4. Does your name have a meaning? If so, what does it mean?
5. Do you think your name is a good name for the opposite gender too, or for only one gender? Explain your reasons.
6. Do you like your name? Why, or why not?

B | Organizing Ideas. Prepare to tell the class about your partner's name. Organize your notes from exercise **A** in a chart like the one below.

Name	Notes
Paulina	father chose it, father's name=Paul

Presentation Skills: Preparing Notes for Speaking

Good notes can help you when you speak in front of the class. To be useful, written notes for speaking should be:

- Short—not complete sentences, only words and phrases to help you remember the most important ideas
- Clearly written in LARGE letters
- Written on a card or small piece of paper that's easy to hold

C | Presentation. Tell the class about your partner's name. Use your notes from exercise **B** to help you.

D | Discussion. Discuss the information you found most interesting, unusual, or surprising about the students in your class and their names.

> I think it's interesting that every male member of Alexandre's family is named *Alexandre.* That could be confusing!

GENDER AND SOCIETY

LESSON A AND B   VIEWING

Wodaabe

In the Wodaabe culture, special clothes and make-up emphasize male attractiveness, which includes white teeth and the ability to cross one's eyes.

The Wodaabe live in parts of Niger, Nigeria, and surrounding parts of western and central Africa.

Before Viewing

A | Critical Thinking. Discuss the questions with a partner.

1. In your culture, how important is physical beauty for women? What are some of the characteristics of feminine beauty in your culture?
2. In your culture, how important is physical beauty for men? What are some of the characteristics of masculine beauty or handsomeness in your culture?
3. Have you ever seen a beauty contest? What happens at a beauty contest? How are the winners chosen?

  B | Using a Dictionary. Read and listen about a beauty contest in the Wodaabe culture. Use context clues or your dictionary to help you understand the underlined words.

The Wodaabe Geerewol Festival

For most of the year, the Wodaabe are <u>nomadic</u>, moving from place to place to find grass for their cattle. For one week each year, however, it's festival time for the Wodaabe. It's called the *geerewol*, and it's a chance for Wodaabe men to <u>show off</u> for the women.

The *geerewol* is a kind of beauty pageant, and the men who participate wear <u>makeup</u> to emphasize the features that are considered beautiful by the Wodaabe: long noses, strong white teeth, and large eyes, among other characteristics.

The *geerewol* is all about <u>attraction</u>—both physical beauty and <u>charm</u>. While the men dance, the women watch and carefully evaluate the men's <u>appearance</u>. When an available woman finds a man who is <u>irresistible</u> to her, she lets him know with small gestures. With many women watching, the pageant has many winners.

While Viewing

A | Note-Taking. Watch the video and take notes in your notebook on your reactions to it.

1. What surprises you?
2. What do you find interesting?
3. What do you have questions about?

B | Watch again and take notes on the following details.

1. Purpose of black lipstick: _____
2. Purpose of yellow makeup: _____
3. Who are the judges? _____
4. Who competes in the *geerewol*? _____

This Wodaabe man in Niger is part of a nomadic tribe that trades and herds animals in western Africa.

After Viewing

Critical Thinking. Discuss the questions with your group.

1. Why do you think psychologists are interested in the Wodaabe and the *geerewol* festival?
2. What does the video tell you (and not tell you) about gender roles in the Wodaabe tribe?
3. Think about what you learned in Lesson A about gender. Do you think that nature or culture has more to do with our ideas about physical beauty? Explain.

Group of Wodaabe men at festival time.

LESSON B | BUILDING VOCABULARY

A | Meaning from Context. Read and listen to the two articles. Notice the words in blue. These are words you will hear and use in Lesson B.

Boys and Girls Test Their Geography

Question: Timis County is located in the western part of which European Country?

Eric Yang knew the answer. "Romania!" he said, and became the winner of the National Geographic Geography Bee. Every year, thousands of young people compete in this international contest of geographical knowledge. Three winners from each country go on to the world championship.

For years, however, the contest's organizers have wondered about a question of their own. An equal number of girls and boys enter the contest at the school and regional levels. Why are so many of the national winners boys? In the United States, Eric's home country, only two girls have won the top prize since 1989.

Teams from seventeen countries competed in this year's National Geographic World Championship in Mexico City.

Canadian Boys Win World Geography Contest

Three boys from Canada have won the National Geographic World Championship in Mexico City, beating 16 other national teams. The second prize went to three boys from the USA, and the third prize to three boys from Poland. All teams also enjoyed several days of sightseeing in Mexico.

As in the past, most contestants were male, and this year two scientists investigated the reasons for this. They concluded that there is in fact a small gender gap in geography, but they couldn't find the cause. Possibly, boys are taught to be more assertive than girls, or they might feel more pressure from their parents. Maybe boys have a better ability to use maps. Or maybe teachers encourage boys more in geography classes.

USING VOCABULARY

B | Match each word in blue from exercise **A** with its definition.

1. level ___
2. equal ___
3. investigate ___
4. conclude ___
5. gap ___
6. possibly ___
7. assertive ___
8. knowledge ___
9. ability ___
10. encourage ___

a. (adj.) the same in number, size, or value
b. (v.) to arrive at an opinion or judgment
c. (adj.) able to give your opinions strongly and clearly
d. (n.) skill that makes it possible to do something
e. (v.) look at something carefully, research
f. (v.) give someone the confidence to do or try something
g. (adv.) maybe
h. (n.) a point on a certain scale, such as quality or ability
i. (n.) a space or difference between two things
j. (n.) the things you know about

C | **Giving Reasons.** Look back at the second newspaper article and write four possible reasons for the "geography gap" between girls and boys. Then write two more ideas of your own.

Reasons from the article:

1. _____
2. _____
3. _____
4. _____

Your own ideas:

1. _____
2. _____

Critical Thinking Focus: Evaluating Reasons

When you read or hear reasons for something, it's important to ask yourself whether the reasons make sense and are believable based on what you know.

D | **Critical Thinking.** Compare your ideas in exercise **A** with your partner's ideas. What do you think is the best explanation for the gap?

E | **Discussion.** Talk about the elementary school subjects below with a partner. Which ones did you have the most ability in? Did your teachers and parents encourage you in these subjects? Did they pressure you to do well? Do you think there is a gender gap in any of these subjects? Explain your reasons.

science   reading and writing
history   foreign languages
art   mathematics
geography

GENDER AND SOCIETY | 15

LESSON B DEVELOPING LISTENING SKILLS

A firefighter

Before Listening

 Discuss the questions as a class.

1. Which jobs in your country are done mostly by women? mostly by men?
2. Have the jobs that men and women do changed over time?

Listening: A Conversation between Classmates

 A | **Listening for Main Ideas.** Listen to the first part of the conversation and answer the questions.

1. What did Dylan do over the summer?
   _____
2. What did Mia do over the summer?
   _____
3. What class are they taking together?
   _____
4. What do you think Dylan will talk about next?
   _____

 B | Listen to the next part of the conversation and circle the correct answers.

1. Dylan thinks that women firefighters _____.
   a. are a bad idea
   b. are a good idea
   c. don't exist
2. Mia believes that _____.
   a. all men are stronger than all women
   b. some men are stronger than some women
   c. most men are stronger than most women
3. Mia's drawing looks like _____.
   a. graph A
   b. graph B
   c. graph C

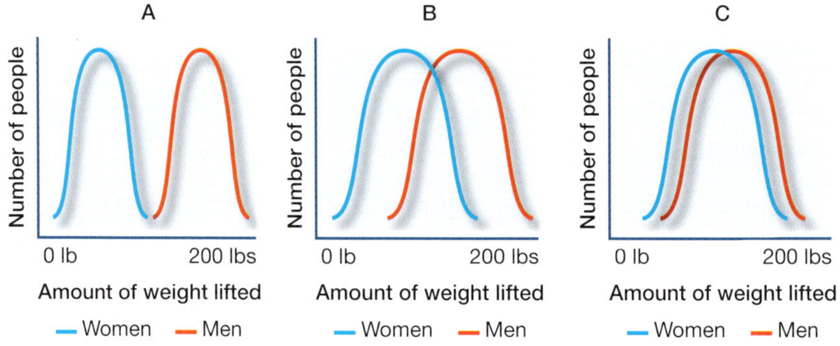

A flight attendant

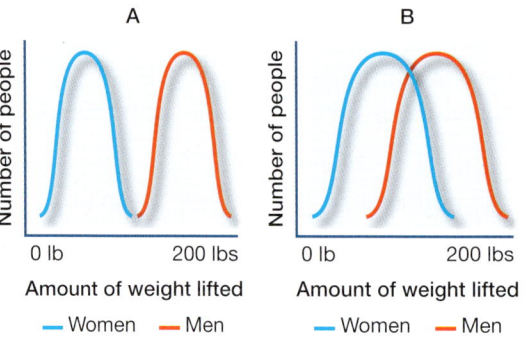

16 | UNIT 1

C | Listening for Details. Read the statements. Then listen to the last part of the conversation and circle **T** for *true* or **F** for *false*.

1. Mia thinks that women should take jobs away from men.   T   F
2. Mia's aunt liked working as a flight attendant.   T   F
3. Dylan thinks being a flight attendant would be interesting.   T   F
4. Dylan thinks men aren't good flight attendants.   T   F
5. Mia is angry with Dylan.   T   F

After Listening

Collaboration. Complete the activities below with a partner.

1. Talk about the three graphs on the previous page. Can you think of other characteristics of men and women that fit these patterns?
2. Make your own graph about a gender difference, similar to one of the graphs on the previous page. Label the parts.
3. Draw your graph on the board and explain it to the class. Does everyone agree with you?

Pronunciation

Can/Can't

The words *can* and *can't* have very similar pronunciations, but they receive different stress in a sentence. Usually, *can* is not stressed, so the vowel receives a reduced pronunciation. Listen to the difference:

I **can** speak three languages.
We **can't** find our new classroom.

Paying attention to this difference can help you understand these words better.

Listen to these sentences from the conversation again and complete them with *can* or *can't*. Then take turns reading them to a partner.

1. But I _____ also see that I disagree with her about a lot of things.
2. A small woman _____ lift more than 20 pounds.
3. And a woman athlete _____ lift 200 pounds.
4. _____ all men lift 200 pounds?
5. I _____ imagine why the airlines didn't want men.
6. Men _____ lift heavier bags for the passengers.

**Student to Student:
Greeting a Friend after a Long Time**

Wow, I haven't seen you in ages! Hey, stranger! Long time, no see! (informal idiom)

GENDER AND SOCIETY | 17

LESSON B EXPLORING SPOKEN ENGLISH

Language Function

Using Inclusive Language

Inclusive language is language that includes both men and women. In speaking and writing academic English, you are expected to use inclusive language as much as you can. Some important points:

1. Don't use words like *man, he, him,* or *his* to refer to all people.
   X *The average student worries about his exam scores.*
   The average student worries about exam scores.

2. Don't use job titles that refer to only one gender.
   X *That book was written for salesmen.*
   That book was written for salespeople.

3. Don't mention gender if it isn't important.
   X *I had a meeting with a lady engineer this morning.*
   I had a meeting with an engineer this morning.

A | Replace the crossed-out job titles with the correct form of one of the titles from the box.

chair	flight attendant	nurse	business executive
firefighter	mail carrier	server	salesperson

1. Many ~~businessmen~~ _____ travel a lot for their work.
2. The ~~mailman~~ _____ usually comes to my house at about ten o'clock.
3. In the hospital, a very kind ~~male nurse~~ _____ took care of me.
4. The ~~chairman~~ _____ asked the people at the meeting to give their suggestions.
5. I think our ~~waitress~~ _____ provided excellent service. Let's leave a big tip.
6. Being a good listener is an important characteristic for a ~~salesman~~ _____ to have.

B | **Discussion.** With a partner, talk about the following sentences. Does each sentence use inclusive language? If not, rewrite it in your notebook using more inclusive language.

1. The hotel rooms have special features for businessmen and businesswomen, such as extra-large desks.
2. A patient should always ask a doctor for his advice before starting an exercise program.
3. Two of the most popular new movies in this country were made by female directors.
4. Early man lived in caves and wore clothes made from animal skins.
5. Mothers should feed their children plenty of fruits and vegetables.

C | Discussion. Form a group with two or three other students. Look at the job titles from exercise **A** on page 18. Discuss what skills and characteristics make someone successful at each of these professions. Practice using inclusive language as you discuss your ideas.

> A good server is polite to their customers.

Language Function

Talking about Rules and Expectations in the Past

We use the following expressions to talk about rules in the past.
*Female flight attendants **were required** to be very thin.*
*They **had to** stop working when they were 32.*
*They **weren't allowed** to keep their jobs if they gained weight.*
*They **were forbidden** to get married.*
*Female flight attendants **couldn't** get married if they wanted to keep their jobs.*

We use the following language to talk about expectations in the past.
*Stewardesses **were supposed** to be attractive.*
*They **were expected** to be friendly and polite.*

A | Think about men and women in your country 100 years ago. What was different? Complete the sentences with your own ideas.

1. Women were expected to _____.
2. Women were not supposed to _____.
3. Men were not expected to _____.
4. Men were supposed to _____.

 B | Discuss your answers from exercise **A** with your partner.

 C | Think about some of the rules your parents had for you when you were a child. Discuss the questions with your group.

1. Talk about some of the rules your parents had for you when you were in elementary school.
2. Were the rules the same for your older and younger siblings?
3. Were the rules the same for boys and girls in your family?

> I wasn't allowed to ride my bicycle alone.

UNIT 1

ENGAGE: Participating in a Mini-Debate

You are going to have a mini-debate about where gender differences come from. Your teacher will assign you and your partner one of the opinions below (it might not be your opinion). You and your partner will work together to make an argument that supports your opinion.

Opinion 1: Gender differences come mostly from our biology, not our culture.

Opinion 2: Gender differences come mostly from our culture, not our biology.

A | Brainstorming. Brainstorm reasons to support your opinion. Write your ideas in your notebook.

> In some cultures boys and girls are expected to follow different rules.

> In my country parents give their sons and daughters really different kinds of toys.

B | Collaboration. Look at the list of reasons from exercise **A**. Decide which three reasons best support your opinion and write them in the outline below Then think of at least one example to support each of your reasons.

Opinion: _____

Reason 1: _____
Examples: _____
Reason 2: _____
Examples: _____
Reason 3: _____
Examples: _____

C | Note-Taking. Form a group with a student pair that discussed the opposite opinion. Present your opinion and your reasons and examples that support it. Listen to the other pair present their opinion and take notes on their reasons and ideas.

> Gender differences come mostly from our biology, because very young boys and girls already like different kinds of toys.

D | Discussion. Work with your original partner from exercises **A** and **B**. Look at your notes from exercise **B**. Discuss the reasons and examples the other pair talk about to support their opinion. Think of arguments against their reasons.

E | Organizing Ideas. Make notes on your strongest arguments from exercise **D**. Then decide which order you will present them.

F | Presentation. Form a group with the other pair of students again. Take turns presenting your arguments against each other's opinions and reasons.

Reproducing Life

UNIT 2

ACADEMIC PATHWAYS

Lesson A: Listening to a Conversation about a Documentary
Discussing Species Conservation
Lesson B: Listening to a Conversation between Classmates
Creating and Presenting a Group Plan

Think and Discuss

1. Young polar bears are called "cubs." What are some other young animals called?
2. Where do these polar bears live? What other kinds of animals do you think live there?

A polar bear mother and her cubs cuddle together for warmth. These polar bears live in Churchill, Canada.

Exploring the Theme:
Reproducing Life

Look at the photos and read the captions. Then discuss the questions.

1. Which species of animal in the photos interests you the most? Why?
2. What types of reproduction are discussed on these pages?
3. How is reproduction a challenge for these penguins?

Three Types of Reproduction

Plants reproduce through a process called **pollination**. Pollination involves the transfer of a powder called pollen from one plant to another. Insects like this bee are important to the pollination process for some plants.

These Amazon molly fish clone (or copy) themselves naturally. Other types of **cloning** can only take place in scientific laboratories.

The quetzal, like all species of birds, **lays eggs**. Young quetzals become independent in just a few weeks.

Case Study: The King Penguins of Possession Island

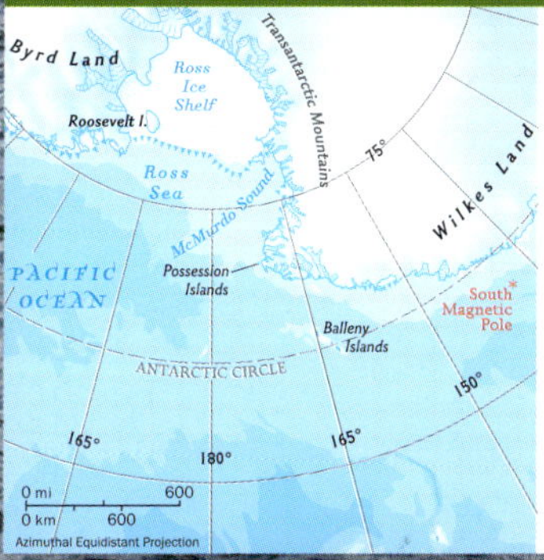

For the penguins of Possession Island, reproduction can be a challenge. The island is crowded and each pair of penguins needs its own territory—a small area of land. Penguins lay eggs and have to keep them warm, which is very difficult in this harsh, cold climate. They must also watch out for predators, since other animals might want to eat their eggs or chicks (baby penguins). Penguins live in large groups called colonies. The largest colony on Possession Island contains 100,000 penguins!

LESSON A — BUILDING VOCABULARY

 A | **Meaning from Context.** Look at the photos and read and listen to the captions. Notice the words in blue. These are words you will hear and use in Lesson A.

The King Penguin: Challenges to Reproduction

An elephant seal shares South Georgia Island with a huge **colony** of King Penguins. The penguins have come to the island to reproduce, but space can be a problem. Each penguin must defend its **territory**, a small area less than three feet (one meter) across.

Although adult King Penguins **weigh** around 30 pounds (14 kilograms), they cannot always **defend** their chicks against **predators** such as this skua. In the ocean, seals and other sea animals sometimes eat penguins.

Cold temperatures also challenge penguin **reproduction**. This **adult** penguin keeps its egg warm until its **mate** returns. Adults may swim and eat for two weeks or more before they return and take over the care of the egg.

Climate change is creating another **challenge**. Penguin chicks are not independent. They **depend** on their parents for food. Warmer ocean water means less food nearby, so penguin parents are away for longer time periods and more chicks die.

B | Write each word in blue next to its definition.

1. _Adult_ (n.) a person or animal that has finished growing
2. _weigh_ (adj.) to have a certain weight
3. _depend_ (adj.) to need (for support)
4. _defend_ (v.) to take action in order to protect something
5. _predator_ (n.) animals that eat other animals
6. _colony_ (n.) a group of animals living together in a certain area
7. _mate_ (n.) an animal's partner in reproduction
8. _territory_ (n.) an area of land that belongs to a certain animal
9. _reproduction_ (n.) the creation of babies
10. _challenge_ (n.) something difficult that requires effort

USING VOCABULARY

A | Read the article and fill in each blank with a word from the box.

colonies   territory   mate   adult

A Land of Kings

It's summer in the southern hemisphere, and time for ____adult____ King Penguins to leave the water and lay their eggs. First, however, each penguin must find a ____mate____.

On Possession Island, there are plenty of penguins to choose from in six different penguin ____colonies____. When photographer Stefano Unterthiner visited the largest one, he saw 100,000 penguins. Each one was defending its ____territory____, a small area less than three feet (one meter) across. Said Unterthiner, "The penguins looked very organized, almost like they were in military formation, each guarding its ground."

"Penguins can seem like fish," says photographer Unterthiner, "but here they truly are birds flying in water."

B | Read the statements. Circle **T** for *true* or **F** for *false* using the information from the article.

1. Possession Island is in the northern hemisphere.   T   **F** → southern
2. The island's largest penguin **colony** has 10,000 birds in it.   T   **F**
3. Each penguin has a large **territory** on the island.   T   **F** small
4. **Adult** penguins leave the water in the winter.   T   **F**
5. Penguins on the island live in six large groups.   **T**   F

C | **Critical Thinking.** Write answers to the following questions.

1. Which probably **weighs** more—**adult** penguins or penguin chicks?
   adult penguins are weighs more.
2. What do you think is the greatest **challenge** to penguin **reproduction**?
   Cold temperatures b/c adult penguin have to keep its egg warm
3. What are some penguin **predators** you know about? (Is a penguin ever a predator?)
   seals, whale
4. What kinds of **predators** do you think penguins have to **defend** their chicks against?
   skua, seals and other sea animals
5. Do you still **depend** on your parents and other family members for some things?
   Yes, I do. I still depend on my parents for living fee in Toronto

D | With a partner, take turns asking and answering the questions in exercise **C**.

REPRODUCING LIFE | 25

LESSON A — DEVELOPING LISTENING SKILLS

Before Listening

A | Meaning from Context. Read and listen about a new film about penguins. Notice the underlined words.

The Penguins of Possession Island

This is not the only <u>documentary film</u> about penguins this year, but it is one of the year's best. In this beautiful nature documentary, King Penguins come to Possession Island to find mates. Most of the <u>footage</u>[1] shows us penguins on land, but some footage shows us penguins in the water.

There is something in this documentary for everyone—except perhaps for young children. Some <u>scenes</u> of penguin chicks being killed by predators are difficult to watch—even for adults.

I was lucky enough to see *The Penguins of Possession Island* in a movie theater, and everyone in the <u>audience</u> liked the film. Don't miss your chance to see it, even if you have to watch it on TV.

B | Choose the correct ending for each sentence below.

1. *Film* is another word for _____.
   a. movie   b. television
2. A documentary film shows us _____.
   a. a fictional story   b. something from real life
3. Film footage comes from a _____.
   a. camera   b. book
4. The scenes in a film are _____.
   a. small parts of the film   b. the music in the film
5. People in the audience _____.
   a. make a film   b. watch a film

Listening: A Conversation about a Documentary

A | Listening for Main Ideas. Listen and choose the best answer to the questions.

1. Who do you think the speakers probably are?
   a. They're friends.   b. They're co-workers.   c. They're classmates.
2. What are the speakers doing?
   a. Choosing film footage   b. Adding sound to a film   c. Talking to a photographer

B | Listening for Details. Listen again. In your notebook, write the answers to the questions.

1. How much footage from Possession Island do the speakers have?
2. What does the man say about the predator birds?
3. Why does the man want to include footage of the photographers?
4. Why doesn't the woman want to include winter scenes?
5. How long will the finished film be?

[1]**Footage** of something is film of it.

After Listening

Critical Thinking Focus: Judging the Relevance of Information

The speakers in the listening passage had a story to tell. In order to do this, they needed to judge and select film footage that was relevant to their story, in other words—footage that was directly connected with their story.

A | Which footage did the speakers choose? Label each idea below **R** (relevant) or **NR** (not relevant).

_____ King Penguins finding their mates

_____ Penguins swimming in the water

_____ Winter on the island

_____ Challenges that the penguins face

_____ Parents feeding chicks

A photographer uses an underwater camera to film this coral reef in Fiji.

B | **Discussion.** Imagine that you and your partner are choosing footage for a new documentary film. You want to show the negative effects of global warming on ocean life.

1. Which footage connects to your story? Label each scene below **R** (relevant) or **NR** (not relevant).

   _____ A scientist explaining how global warming causes changes in the ocean

   _____ A marine biologist talking about damage to coral reefs due to warmer water

   _____ A farmer talking about dry conditions due to climate change

   _____ A fish swimming, but finding little food to eat due to warmer water

   _____ A beachfront hotel owner who is happy about the longer summer tourist season

   _____ A walrus eating food on land that was covered by ice a few years ago

A walrus is a large, fat sea mammal.

C | **Collaboration.** With a partner, plan your own documentary film. Follow the steps below. Take notes in your notebook.

1. Choose a species of animal or plant as your topic.
2. Decide what aspect of the animal or plant's life your documentary will be about (reproduction, eating habits, predators, etc.).
3. Decide what kind of footage you will need for your documentary.

D | **Presentation.** Form a group with another pair of students and talk about your ideas for a documentary. Explain how your film footage is relevant to your story.

REPRODUCING LIFE | 27

LESSON A EXPLORING SPOKEN ENGLISH

Dolly the sheep, was the first mammal cloned from an adult cell.

This baby mammoth is a member of an extinct species. Its DNA was preserved by the cold and ice of Siberia.

Pronunciation

Stress Patterns Before Suffixes

When some suffixes are added to words, they change the syllable stress pattern.

educate ⟶ edu**ca**tion
romance ⟶ ro**man**tic

(See page 209 in the Independent Student Handbook for more information on suffixes.)

A | Listen to each word and circle the syllable with the strongest stress.

genetic   technical   reproduction

B | Underline the suffix in each word from exercise **A**. What do you notice about stress before suffixes in the words from exercise **A**?

C | Practice saying the words in the chart below. Underline the stressed syllables. Notice the stress patterns and write the part of speech of –ic, -ical, and -tion. Then compare your answers with a partner's.

Suffix: -ic	Suffix: -ical	Suffix: -tion
Part of Speech: _____	Part of Speech: _____	Part of Speech: _____
genetic	ethical	extinction
specific	practical	connection
problematic	mechanical	conservation
characteristic	psychological	reproduction

D | Look at the flow chart on page 29 and listen to information about cloning animals. Circle each word in the box when you hear it.

reproduction   genetic   information   chemicals

28 | UNIT 2

Figure 1.1: Cloning from an Adult Cell

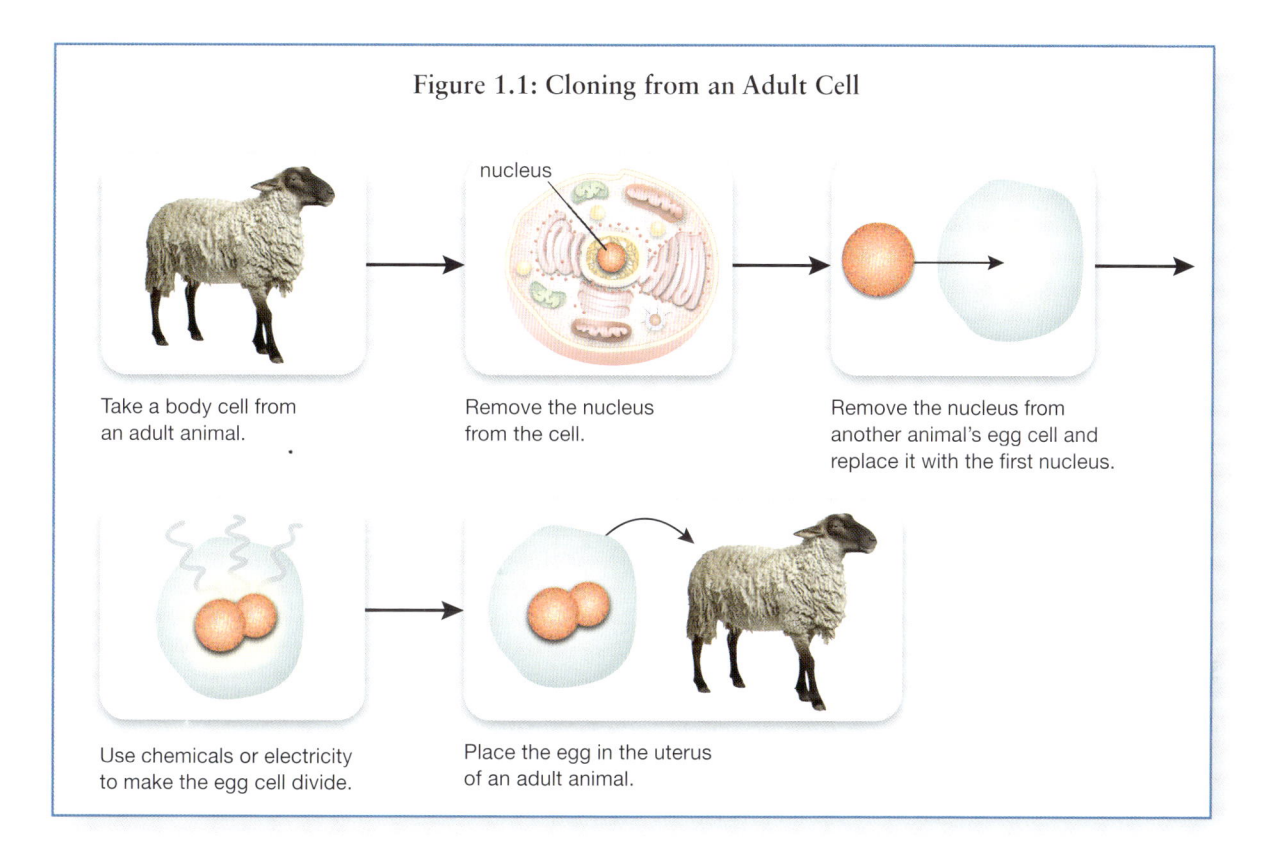

Take a body cell from an adult animal.

Remove the nucleus from the cell.

Remove the nucleus from another animal's egg cell and replace it with the first nucleus.

Use chemicals or electricity to make the egg cell divide.

Place the egg in the uterus of an adult animal.

Language Function

Explaining a Process

We use transition words like *then* and *next* when explaining the steps of a process.

A | Listen to the information about cloning animals again. Take notes on the words and phrases the speaker uses to transition from one step to the next in the process.

B | Take turns explaining the cloning process to a partner. Use the transition words from exercise **A** and the information from the flow chart.

C | **Discussion.** Form a group with two or three other students and discuss the questions.

1. Cloning could be used to bring animals back from extinction. Should extinct animals such as the mammoth be brought back through cloning?
2. In Europe, the auroch—a very large, extinct form of cattle—could be brought back to help with forest conservation. The aurochs ate beech trees, which are now too numerous in Europe's forests. Should aurochs be brought back to help other tree species survive?

Scottish Highland cattle will be used in efforts to clone aurochs.

LESSON A

Grammar

Adjective Clauses

An adjective clause describes or modifies a noun—just as an adjective does. We can form a complex sentence with an adjective clause from two simple sentences:
I have a sister. My sister works at the airport. = *I have a sister **who** works at the airport.*
                                                                  noun   adjective clause

In this sentence, the adjective clause describes the noun *sister*.

In subject adjective clauses, the relative pronoun replaces the subject. The subject relative pronouns are: *who, that,* and *which*.
A skua is a type of bird. ***A skua*** *eats penguins.* = *A skua is a type of bird **that** eats penguins.*

In object adjective clauses, the relative pronoun replaces an object. The object relative pronouns are: *that, which,* and *whom* (or *who* in informal speech).
*I took the class. Professor Riley taught **the class.*** = *I took the class **that** Professor Riley taught.*

Note: When the relative pronoun is an object, it can sometimes be omitted.
I took the class Professor Riley taught.

A | Choose the correct relative pronoun in each sentence below.

1. A cell's nucleus is the part (who/that) contains DNA.
2. Dolly was the first mammal (that/whom) was cloned successfully.
3. It was the first thing (who/that) I learned in Chemistry 101.
4. There are two main predators (that/who) penguins must deal with.
5. Do you know the man (who/which) is wearing the white shirt?
6. We're watching the documentary film (whom/that) our professors made.

B | **Critical Thinking.** Complete each sentence using any appropriate adjective clause.

1. Cloning is a type of reproduction _that does not require a male/happens in a laboratory/etc._ .
2. An island is a piece of land that _____.
3. Stefano Unterthiner is a photographer who _____.
4. I enjoy films that _____.
5. She's the biologist who _____.

C | **Discussion.** Think about the topics below. Then discuss with a partner. Practice using adjective clauses.

1. Interesting facts about your family members or friends
2. Interesting facts you know about animals

> Platypuses are mammals that lay eggs.

SPEAKING

Discussing Species Conservation

A | Read the information below.

> Over time, many species of plants and animals have become extinct. This has happened for many different reasons, but nowadays human beings are often the cause of species extinction. In this section, you will discuss species conservation and the causes of extinction.

B | **Discussion.** Discuss the following question in a small group. How can each of the following lead to species extinction?

- Hunting and fishing
- Logging (cutting down trees)
- Farming
- Global warming and climate change
- An increasing human population

Panda bears are just one of the earth's endangered species.

C | **Presentation.** Report some of your group's ideas to the rest of the class.

D | **Critical Thinking.** Discuss the following arguments in favor of species conservation with a partner. Then rank the arguments from 1 (most relevant) to 4 (least relevant).

_____ Some popular endangered animals provide economic benefits (e.g., ecotourism).
_____ The extinction of one plant or animal can affect other plants and animals.
_____ Some species could be beneficial for human health and medicine.
_____ Genetic diversity (a wide variety of living things) makes it possible for plants and animals to evolve and change.

E | **Discussion.** Form a group with two or three other students, and try to agree on the best way to finish each sentence below.

1. We (should/shouldn't) clone species that have become extinct because . . .
2. We (should/shouldn't) spend our time and energy on species conservation because . . .

Student to Student: Asking for Repetition

Use these expressions in informal conversations when you need to ask for repetition.

I'm sorry? *What's that?*
I didn't catch what you said. *I missed that.*

LESSON A AND B VIEWING

TURTLE EXCLUDER

Before Viewing

A | Critical Thinking. In Lesson A of this unit, you talked about species conservation. In this video, you will learn about a low-tech way to conserve the Kemp's Ridley sea turtle. Before you watch, discuss the questions below with a partner.

1. Nowadays, the Kemp's Ridley sea turtle is seldom eaten by people, yet it has become an endangered species—partly due to fishing in the Gulf of Mexico. Why do you think this is happening?
2. What are some other threats to sea animals besides fishing?

B | Self-Reflection. Discuss these questions with a partner. Do you eat fish or seafood? If so, what kind do you like? Does fishing for these species cause any environmental problems?

C | Using Adjective Clauses. Work with a partner. Match the sentence beginnings to their endings. Pay attention to the underlined words. Use your dictionary to help you.

1. ___ We usually exclude things that . . .
2. ___ A biologist is someone . . .
3. ___ A device is something that . . .
4. ___ A population is a group of animals that . . .
5. ___ Sharks, fish, and shrimp are animals . . .

a. all live in one place.
b. that live in the sea.
c. we don't want.
d. has a special function.
e. who studies living things.

While Viewing

A | Watch the video. Then answer the questions below.

1. What is the Turtle Excluder?
   _____

2. In your own words, how does the Turtle Excluder work?
   _____
   _____

3. In the U.S., what kind of fishermen must use the Turtle Excluder?
   _____

B | **Note-Taking.** Watch the video again and fill in the T-chart below.

Disadvantage to Fishermen (according to some fishermen)	Advantage to Fishermen (according to biologists)

A fisherman releases a cascade of shrimp onto the deck of his boat.

Although both men and women fish, *fisherman* is still a very common word. In the future, we may use the word "fisher" instead.

After Viewing

Collaboration. Imagine that you are part of a public relations group. As a group, it's your job to convince fishermen that the Turtle Excluder is good for everyone. Follow the steps below.

1. Brainstorm several benefits of a healthy sea turtle population. Besides the advantages you identified in exercise **B** above, consider the environment, tourism, the future, and any other topics you can think of.

2. Write a letter to send to all the fishermen in the Gulf of Mexico. This letter should make the fishermen feel good about using the Turtle Excluder.

A Turtle Excluder device

REPRODUCING LIFE | 33

LESSON B   BUILDING VOCABULARY

A | **Meaning from Context.** Read and listen to the information about orchids. Notice the words in blue. These are words you will hear and use in Lesson B.

Orchid Question & Answer

Q: Imagine that you're a flower. Like every other living thing, you want to reproduce. But you can't move! How can you get your DNA to another flower?

A: Offer food. This is a great way to **trick** birds or **insects**. They think they're just getting a free meal in the form of nectar, a sweet liquid. However, they're also carrying your **pollen**—a substance that contains your DNA—to the next flower that they visit.

Q: Nectar is full of calories, so it requires a lot of energy to produce. Is there a less "expensive" way for me to move my pollen around?

A: Absolutely! Many orchids[1] have found **fascinating** ways to **attract** insects without offering any food. To do this, they **imitate** something that the insects want. Here are some ways they do this:

Shelter: Even insects need a place to live. Some orchids **resemble** insect burrows.[2] The insects crawl in, but since it's not really a good place to live, they leave with pollen on their bodies.

Scents: Insects are attracted to the smell of food, so orchids produce scents that seem wonderful to bugs, but not always to humans. The *Dracula* orchid attracts tiny insects called gnats by smelling like a dirty diaper!

Food: Orchids don't need to offer real food as long as they seem to offer food. The *Epidendrum* orchid resembles milkweed, a favorite food of butterflies. Butterflies visit the plant, but all they **obtain** is pollen to carry away when they leave.

Mates: One of the most common orchid tricks is to offer the promise of a mate. The flower of the *Ophrys* orchid in Italy resembles the wings of a female bee. It even smells like a female bee, so **instinct** tells every male bee in the area to visit the plant.

Hummingbird getting food from an orchid

Butterfly on an Epidendrum orchid in Panama

B | Use context clues to write each word in blue in the correct box below.

Nouns	Verbs	Adjectives
insects, shelter, scents, instinct	trick, attract, imitate, resemble = look like, obtain = get	fascinating = very interesting

[1] **Orchids** are flowering plants in the family *orchidaceae*.
[2] **Burrows** are small holes where insects can live.

USING VOCABULARY

A | Using a Dictionary. With a partner, fill in each blank with the correct form of a vocabulary word from exercise **B**. Use each word only once, and use your dictionary to help you with words you are not sure about. Then complete each sentence with your own ideas.

1. Please close the window. The smell of the cake is _attracting bees._
2. I'm interested in many subjects at school, but the most _fascinating_ subject for me is _English_.
3. We tried to borrow money from the bank, but we couldn't _obtain_ a loan because _they didn't believe us_.
4. Many people dislike _insects_, but bees are _exception useful_.
5. Don't send them your bank account number! It's a _trick_. They're really _suspicious (= doubtful)_.
6. I don't like the _scent_ of that flower. To me, it smells like _garbage_.
7. Birds need a safe place for their eggs, so the best kind of _shelter_ for them is _nest_.
8. Baby crocodiles never see their parents. They must use their _instincts_ to _exist / survive_.
9. She doesn't look like her mother at all, but she does _resemble her father_.
10. You need to develop your own artistic style, so don't _imitate_ other artists' _work_.

B | Critical Thinking. Discuss the following questions in a group then share some of your ideas with the rest of the class.

1. In your culture, which characteristics help a person to **attract** a mate?
2. People use perfume because the **scent** can be very attractive. What other **tricks** do people use to make themselves more attractive?
3. In the animal world, a mate that can offer food and **shelter** might be very attractive. Is that true in the human world as well?
4. Animals have **instincts**, and these **instincts** cause certain behaviors that help the animals survive. Do human beings also have **instincts**, or do we only think and reason?

LESSON B | DEVELOPING LISTENING SKILLS

Before Listening

Emphasis on Key Words

Some words in a sentence or in a conversation receive more stress or emphasis than other words. Look at the information below. Then complete the activities that follow.

Growing orchids in a greenhouse

Content Words	Content words carry the most meaning in a sentence. They include nouns, verbs, and sometimes other words. He **told** me he was **finished** with the **assignment**. Is that a **cow** in the **road**?
New Information	When a speaker puts extra emphasis, or stress, on new information in a conversation, the listener can follow the ideas more easily. A: What did the professor tell you? B: Nothing, because I talked to the **secretary**. A: **Which** secretary? B: The secretary in the **botany department**.

A | Read part of a conversation between two university students. Underline the words and phrases that you think will get extra emphasis.

> Leo: Hi, Elena. Are you on your way to the greenhouse?
> Elena: Hi, Leo. Yes, I am.
> Leo: Good. We can walk there together. Have you been to the greenhouse before?
> Elena: I have. It's a fascinating place—to me, anyway.
> Leo: Oh, I totally agree. They have plants from all over the world—even tropical plants.

B | Listen and check your predictions from exercise **A**.

Listening: A Conversation between Classmates

A | Listening for Main Ideas. Listen to the whole conversation and choose the best answer.

1. What was the last lecture about?
   a. Greenhouses
   b. Orchids
   c. Tropical plants
2. What is special about epiphytes?
   a. They don't need sunlight to grow.
   b. They don't grow in the ground.
   c. They don't have any predators.

A male sand bee is attracted to this Italian orchid's flowers, which resemble a female sand bee.

B | Listening for Details. Listen again and answer the questions about epiphytes.

1. How do epiphytes obtain water?

   _____

2. Where do epiphytes grow?

   _____

3. Why do epiphytes grow there?

   _____

4. How are epiphytes able to grow there?

   _____

5. What's the connection between orchids and epiphytes?

   _____

After Listening

Self-Reflection. Discuss the following questions with a partner.

1. Are you comfortable talking with people whom you don't know very well? Explain.
2. The speakers in the listening passage didn't know each other well, but they did have a good conversation. Check the things the speakers had in common to talk about.

   ❑ Their class schedules   ❑ The greenhouses   ❑ Knowledge of orchids
   ❑ A class lecture   ❑ Knowledge of   ❑ Knowledge of
                                     epiphytes   houseplants

3. What do you and your partner have in common? Find a topic and have a friendly conversation for at least two minutes.

REPRODUCING LIFE

LESSON B EXPLORING SPOKEN ENGLISH

Language Function

Making Suggestions

There are several ways to make polite suggestions. You can be less direct or more direct depending on the situation and how strongly you feel about your suggestion.

Less direct We **could meet** after class to talk about the assignment.
Why don't you **call** him and find out?

More direct I **recommend talking** to your professor.
I **suggest** that you **talk** to your professor.
Let's get together at the coffee shop this afternoon.

Although we usually use **should** to give advice, it can also be used for suggestions.
Maybe you **should** send her a text message.

Grammar Note: The verbs *recommend* and *suggest* are transitive verbs. Their objects can be:

1. nouns   I recommend **hot tea**.
2. gerunds   I suggest **taking** the bus.
3. noun clauses I recommend **that we do some research online**.

A | Complete the conversation below with a partner. Use the less direct language from the **Making Suggestions** chart.

Rasa: Bob isn't doing well in the class. What do you think we should do?
Doris: Maybe we _____ help him with his homework.
Rasa: That's a good idea, but the homework usually isn't a group assignment.
Doris: True. He's supposed to do it himself.
Rasa: _____ ask the instructor to talk to Bob.
Doris: Yes, but that's going behind his back. He might not like that.
Rasa: Then _____ talk to Bob about it?
We _____ suggest that he talk to the instructor.
Doris: That's probably the best idea.

B | Practice the conversation with your partner. Then switch roles and practice it again.

38 | UNIT 2

C | Complete the conversation below with a partner. Use the more direct language from the **Making Suggestions** chart. There may be more than one correct answer.

Miguel: What's the matter? You look worried.

Pierre: It's my oldest son. He finished high school, and now he spends all his time watching TV.

Miguel: I _____ telling him to get a job. He needs to earn his own money.

Pierre: That's true, but I really want him to get more education.

Miguel: Then I _____ that you go and visit some universities with him. He might like that.

Pierre: Sure, he'd like that, but then what?

Miguel: _____ introduce him to some of the professional people that we know.

Pierre: That's a good idea. They could tell my son about their careers.

Miguel: Exactly. And he might find something that he wants to do.

D | Practice the conversation with your partner. Then switch roles and practice it again.

E | **Collaboration.** Read the situation below. Then follow the directions.

Situation: You are known as "the problem-solving committee" because you always make good suggestions. Working together with another pair of students, write responses to the following email messages using language from the **Making Suggestions** chart. Then share your responses with the class.

Red panda

To: PSC
Subject: Our red panda pair

Dear Problem-Solving Committee:

We have a problem with the red pandas here at the National Zoo. We have an adult male and an adult female, and they're in the same enclosure together. So far, however, we have no baby red pandas. What do you suggest?

Best,
Dr. Nancy Hartl

To: PSC
Subject: Plant species

Dear Problem-Solving Committee:

When I say, "endangered species," what do you think of? A cute panda bear? Or an unusual kind of fish? Well, they're not the only species in danger. I'm a botanist, and I'm very concerned about the world's plants. Many, many species of plants are endangered—mostly because of human activities such as farming. How can I make the public more aware of this problem?

Thank you,
Mr. Silvio Rhodes

UNIT 2

ENGAGE: Creating and Presenting a Group Plan

You are going to create and present a group plan for studying an endangered species.

A | Form a group with two or three other students and read the information below.

Good news! Your group has received a large research grant to study an endangered species' reproductive behavior. You have plenty of money, so you can travel anywhere and study the species of your choice.

B | Fill out the questionnaire below to decide what species your group will study and where.

Research Project Questionnaire

1. We'd like to study . . .
   - ❏ a plant species.
   - ❏ an animal species.

2. We'd prefer to study . . .
   - ❏ a popular species.
   - ❏ a species that's not well-known.

3. We'd like to travel . . .
   - ❏ to a country that's far away.
   - ❏ within this country.

4. We'd prefer to travel . . .
   - ❏ by plane or helicopter.
   - ❏ by car or boat.

5. We'd like to do . . .
   - ❏ a short study (weeks).
   - ❏ a long study (months).

C | **Organizing Ideas.** Working as a group, make a plan for your study using the form below. Look back at your questionnaire for ideas, and practice making suggestions as you discuss your plan.

Study Plan

Species: _____

Purpose of Study: _____   Length of Study: _____

Study Location: _____   Travel Plans: _____

Presentation Skills: Using Specific Details

Specific details in your presentation help your audience understand your exact meaning. Using adverbs, adjectives, and adjective clauses are good ways to do this.

*The Bengal tiger is the **largest** tiger sub-species, and it's **extremely endangered**. We chose a location **where very few people live**.*

D | **Presentation.** Share some of the details of your study plan with the class. Every person in your group should speak. Then invite the class to ask questions and suggest other ideas for your study. Decide how you will present your plan. You can use the board, paper, or PowerPoint.®

UNIT 3

Human Migration

ACADEMIC PATHWAYS

Lesson A: Listening to a PowerPoint® Lecture
Discussing Case Studies
Lesson B: Listening to a Small Group Discussion
Giving a Group Presentation

Think and Discuss

1. This photo shows Hong Kong at night. What do you know about Hong Kong?
2. Hong Kong is a gateway city, home to people from many other countries. Why do you think so many people from other countries live there?
3. Do you know of any other cities with large foreign-born populations?

Lights fill the sky during Hong Kong's "Symphony of Lights." With approximately 3 million foreign-born residents, Hong Kong is one of the world's major "gateway" cities, or entry points for immigrants.

Exploring the Theme: Human Migration

A | Look at the map and map key. Then answer the questions.

1. What do the circles show? What do the arrows show?
2. What is a gateway city?
3. What information does this map show about your country?

B | Look at the photos and read the captions. Then discuss the questions.

1. For how many years was Ellis Island the entry point for immigrants to the United States?
2. According to the information on these pages, why did people immigrate to Germany? to Saudi Arabia? to Australia?

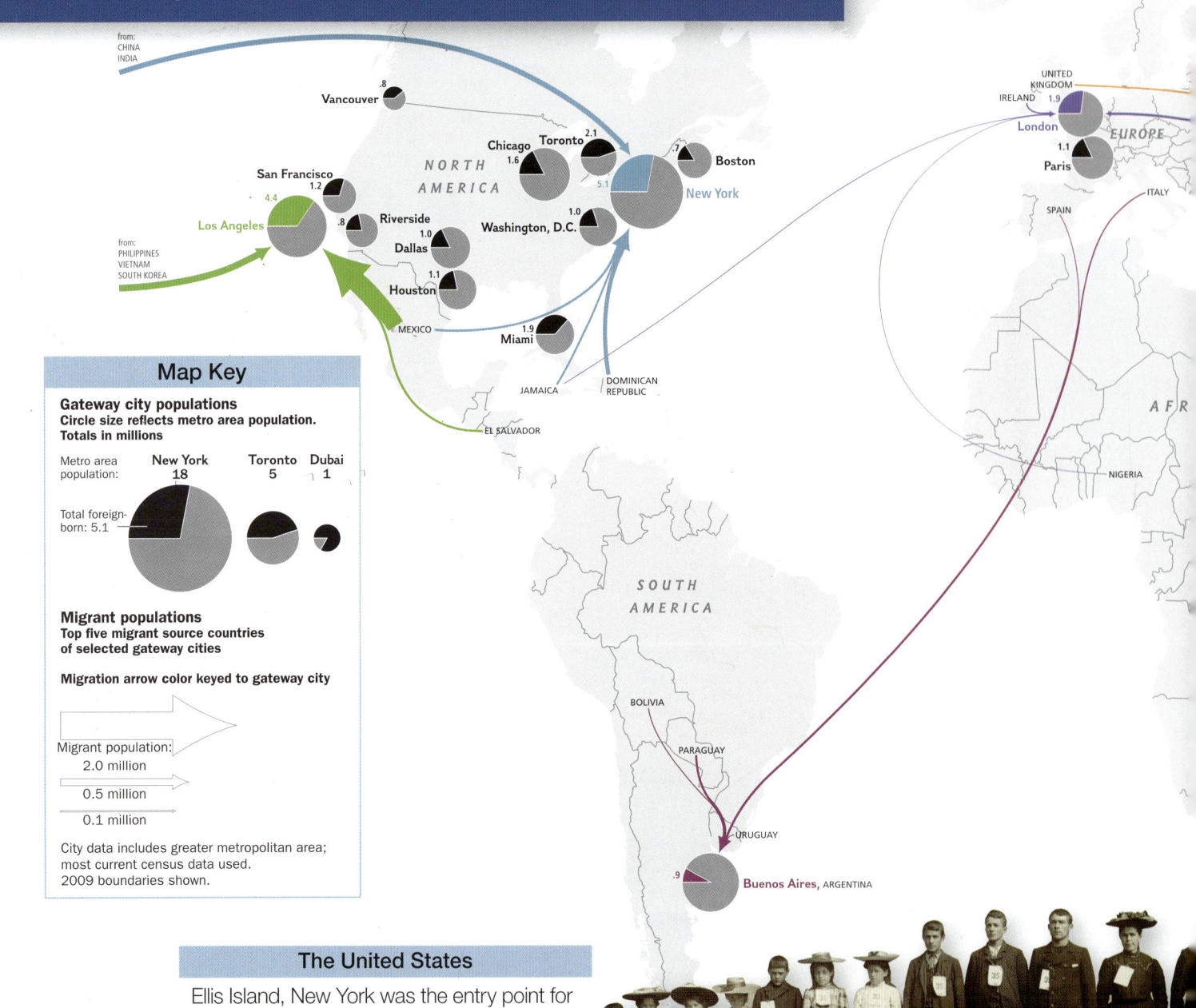

Map Key

Gateway city populations
Circle size reflects metro area population. Totals in millions

Metro area population:
- New York 18 — Total foreign-born: 5.1
- Toronto 5
- Dubai 1

Migrant populations
Top five migrant source countries of selected gateway cities

Migration arrow color keyed to gateway city

Migrant population:
- 2.0 million
- 0.5 million
- 0.1 million

City data includes greater metropolitan area; most current census data used. 2009 boundaries shown.

The United States

Ellis Island, New York was the entry point for immigrants to the United States between the years 1892 to 1924.

42 | UNIT 3

Germany

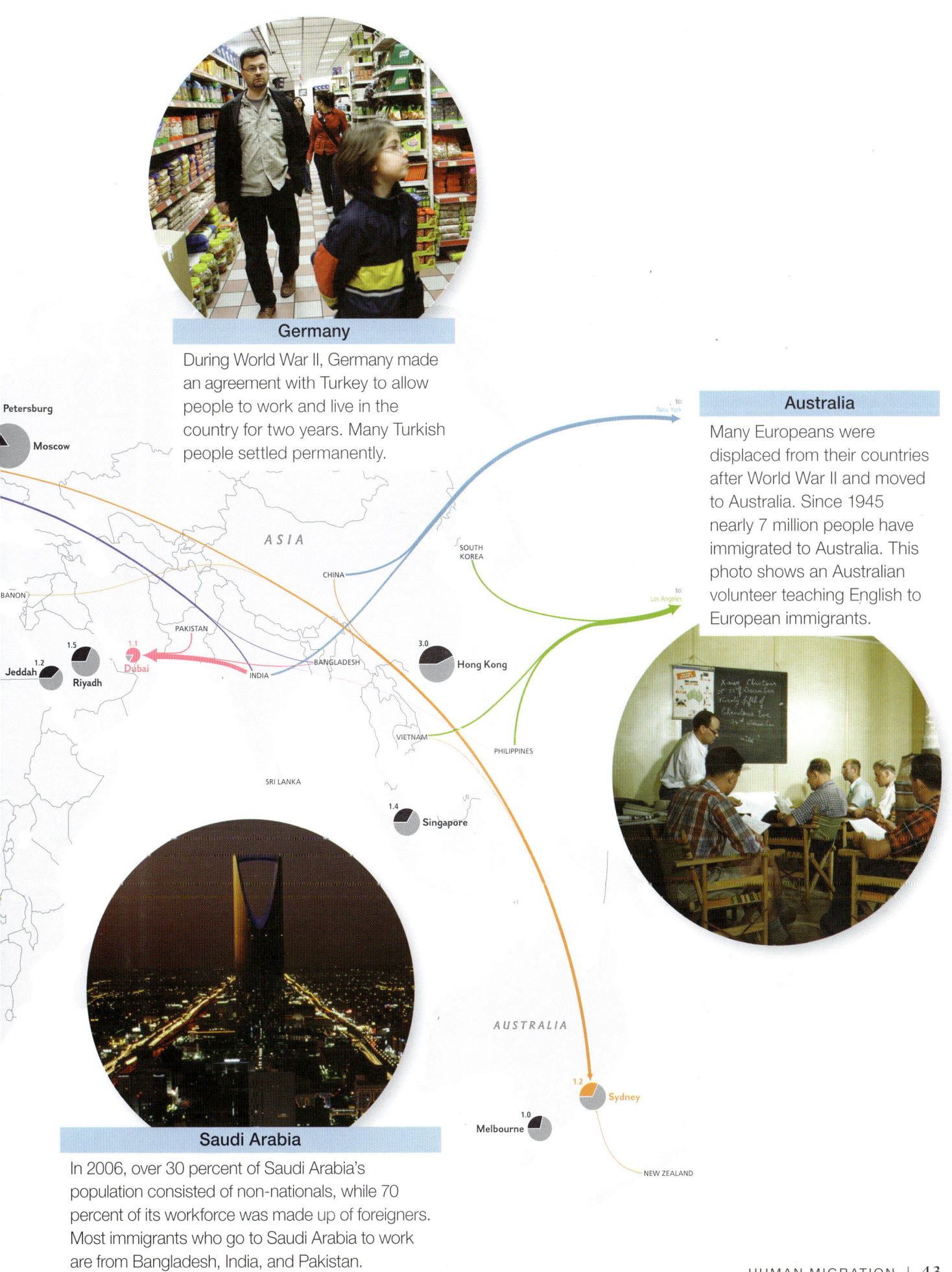

During World War II, Germany made an agreement with Turkey to allow people to work and live in the country for two years. Many Turkish people settled permanently.

Australia

Many Europeans were displaced from their countries after World War II and moved to Australia. Since 1945 nearly 7 million people have immigrated to Australia. This photo shows an Australian volunteer teaching English to European immigrants.

Saudi Arabia

In 2006, over 30 percent of Saudi Arabia's population consisted of non-nationals, while 70 percent of its workforce was made up of foreigners. Most immigrants who go to Saudi Arabia to work are from Bangladesh, India, and Pakistan.

HUMAN MIGRATION | 43

LESSON A
BUILDING VOCABULARY

A | Meaning from Context. Read and listen to the sentences. Then write each word in blue next to its definition below. These are words you will hear and use in Lesson A.

1. Erlinda's native language is Tagalog. She learned English in high school.
2. I have a temporary driver's license. I can use it for two months while I take driving lessons.
3. In the 1840s, more than 8 million people emigrated from Ireland to other countries because there wasn't enough food in Ireland.
4. Our university has programs for students who want to study abroad in France or Mexico.
5. There is a large community of Japanese people who live in São Paulo, Brazil.
6. Many immigrants bring traditions from their home countries to their new countries.
7. I'm working in Hong Kong for two years, but my permanent home is Beijing. I'll go back there to live with my family next year.
8. In my city, there is a trend toward hiring more foreign workers in hotels and restaurants. You can see more people from different countries working in those places.
9. Too many people in my country have negative ideas about foreigners. For example, some people think that foreigners don't work hard and that they can't learn our language.
10. His original job was operating a machine in a factory, but then he graduated from a technical college and now he's an engineer.

a. _trend_ (n.) a general pattern
b. _abroad_ (adv.) out of the country
c. _emigrated_ (v.) to leave your own country to live in another country
d. _temporary_ (adj.) lasting for only a limited time
e. _immigrants_ (n.) a person who comes to live in a new country
f. _permanent_ (adj.) lasting forever
g. _original_ (adj.) first, earliest
h. _negative_ (adj.) bad, unpleasant, or harmful
i. _community_ (n.) a group of people living in a certain place or who are alike in some way
j. _native_ (adj.) related to the place where a person was born

B | Using a Dictionary. Find other forms and definitions of the vocabulary words in your dictionary to complete the chart below.

Vocabulary Word	Related Words	Definitions
immigrant (n.)	v: immigrate	to come to live in a new country
	n: immigration	the process of immigrating
emigrate (v.)	n: _____	a person who emigrates
	n: _____	the process of emigrating
temporary (adj.)	adv: _____	_____
permanent (adj.)	adv: _____	_____
original (adj.)	adv: _____	_____
negative (adj.)	adv: _____	_____
trend (n.)	adj: _____	_____

USING VOCABULARY

A | Look at the photo. Then discuss the questions below with a partner.

1. How would you describe the place where these young women are walking?
2. What do you notice about their clothes?

B | Read the article and fill in each blank with the correct form of a word from exercise **A** on page 44. Use each word only once.

Two young women go for a Sunday afternoon walk in the small town of Budesti, Romania—but their clothes say a lot about an important world (1) _trend_. Along with their traditional Romanian Sunday dresses, the women are wearing fashionable foreign jackets and shoes. People in the women's families went to live (2) _abroad_ to work, and then came back to their hometown, bringing money and foreign products—like these clothes.

More than 2.5 million Romanians have (3) _emigrated_ and are now living in countries such as Spain and Italy. For most of these people, the move is only (4) _temporary_. They plan to work in a store or factory for several years and then return to Romania. They send money to their families and keep in contact with them by phone. Often, they live together in a Romanian (5) _community_ with other people who speak their (6) _native_ language.

Other Romanians have made a (7) _permanent_ move to Canada or Australia and they will never go back to live in their (8) _original_ country. These (9) _immigrants_ often face difficulties in their new country with language, culture, and (10) _negative_ feelings from the local people. But their children usually learn to speak two languages and become comfortable in two cultures.

C | Write down notes to answer the questions below.

1. Are there many **immigrants** in your country? If so, where did they come from? Are most of them **permanent** or **temporary**? _____

2. Do people ever **emigrate** from your country? Why? _____

3. If you had a chance to live **abroad** for 10 years, where would you go? Why, or why not? _____

D | **Discussion.** Form a group with two or three other students and discuss your answers from exercise **C**.

HUMAN MIGRATION | 45

LESSON A | DEVELOPING LISTENING SKILLS

Before Listening

A | Predicting Content. Look at the six slides on pages 46–47 from a professor's lecture about immigration and emigration. What topics do you think the professor will talk about for each slide? Discuss your ideas with a partner. *(See page 202 in the Independent Student Handbook for more information on predicting.)*

B | Form a group with another pair of students and share your predictions.

Listening: A PowerPoint® Lecture

C | Listening for Main Ideas. Listen and number the photos in the order that you hear about them. How many of the topics that you predicted in exercise **A** were in the lecture?

Problems during the 1920s–1930s
1. Several years of very dry, windy weather
2. Economic crisis of the 1930s forced farmers to sell land & leave

North Dakota 100 years ago: had farmland that many immigrants were looking for

North Dakota today: People are leaving, especial rural areas

Modern immigration → People moving to: large cities, not small towns

46 | UNIT 3

Some people trying to preserve the old: ___Communities___

Every year, ___poets___ are invited to this theater in Marmarth.

Importance of the railroad:

1. ___travel was easier___

2. ___when railroad companies building, they sold extra land for cheap___

Town of Corinth, ND

Population in the past: ___75___

Population now: ___6___

🎧 **D | Listening for Details.** Listen again and complete the notes for each slide.
track 1-24

After Listening

Critical Thinking. Discuss the questions with your group.

1. Why did immigrants go to western North Dakota? Why did they leave?
2. Are there places in your country that are losing population? Are the reasons similar to or different from the reasons people left North Dakota?
3. Do you think it's possible to save some of the towns that are disappearing? Should people try to save them?
4. Can you think of any ideas to help the towns that you heard about?

LESSON A   **EXPLORING SPOKEN ENGLISH**

Grammar

Adjectives with *Enough*, *Not Enough*, and *Too*

We use **adjective + enough** to talk about something that is sufficient, or the amount we want.
    *The population is **big enough** to support a grocery store, a gas station, and a café.*

We use **not + adjective + enough** to talk about things that are insufficient, or when there is not the amount we want or need of something.
    *The farm isn't **big enough** to make much money.*

We use **too + adjective** to talk about something that is excessive, or more than we need or want.
    *North Dakota is **too cold** for many people. They prefer to live someplace warmer.*

Too + adjective is often followed by a verb in the infinitive.
    *People believed that North Dakota was **too dry to grow** farm crops.*

A | Write sentences with *too*, *enough*, or *not enough*.

1. I can't go with you tonight. ___I'm too busy to see a movie.___ (I/busy/see a movie)
2. I don't want to live in Marmarth, North Dakota. ___It's too small for me___ (it/small/for me)
3. I can't hear the TV. ___it's not loud enough___ (it's/loud)
4. My children are learning to cook. ___They are old enough to make dinner___ (they/old/make dinner)
5. People don't usually travel to North Dakota. They think ___it's not interesting enough___ (it/interesting/for a vacation)
6. Very few people live in the center of Australia. ___the land is too dry___ (the land/dry)
7. I like this bag. ___it is big enough___ (it/big/ to hold my laptop and my books)

B | Look at the activities below. Can you do these things? Tell a partner. Use an adjective + *enough*, *not enough*, or *too*.

> I'm not fit enough to run 5 miles. What about you?

> I'm too old to run 5 miles!

1. Run 5 miles
2. Buy a new car
3. Study abroad
4. Play chess
5. Take a month-long vacation
6. Get married

C | With your partner, think of three more ideas like the ones in exercise **B**. Then ask another pair of students.

> Can you lift 100 pounds?
>
> I'm not strong enough!

Enough, Not Enough, and Too + Nouns

We use **enough** + **noun** to talk about a sufficient amount of something, or the amount we need or want.
> The local farms are able to produce **enough food** to meet the needs of the population.

We use **not enough** + **noun** to talk about an insufficient amount or lack of something.
> There are **not enough jobs** in the town, so people are leaving.
> I have enough money, but **not enough time.**

We use **too** + **much/many** + **noun** to talk about an excessive amount of something, or more than we want or need.
> My city has **too many** cars and **too much** pollution.

A | Complete the sentences. Use *too much/many, enough,* or *not enough* + noun.

1. Some people emigrate because there is __not enough__ food in their native countries.
2. Many people don't want to live in North Dakota because there is __too much__ snow in the winter.
3. My sister moved to a small town in the country because there was __too much__ crime in the city.
4. The problem with Boston is that there are __too many__ cars, and __not enough__ parking spaces.
5. Do we have __enough__ gas to get all the way to New Haven?

B | **Discussion.** Look at the topics below. Discuss your ideas and opinions about each topic with your group. Use *too, enough,* or *not enough* + nouns in your discussion.

1. Advantages and disadvantages of living in a big city
2. Greatest challenges faced by people in your country
3. Challenges you face in your everyday life

> Living in a small town is nice because it's safe, but there are not enough good jobs or things to do on the weekends.

HUMAN MIGRATION | 49

LESSON A

Language Function

Asking for Reasons

We ask for reasons in order to:

- find out more about a topic we are interested in
- get information and details we need for a research project, etc.
- keep a conversation going, or show interest in what a speaker is talking about

Here are some ways of asking for reasons.

Why is that?
What is/are the reason(s) for that?
Really, why/why not?

What do you think the reason is for that?
That's interesting. Why not?/Why is that?

A | Fill out the questionnaire about immigration and emigration. Write two more questions of your own.

Question	Yes	No	Reason
1. Do many people emigrate from your country?	X	X	Not enough jobs, too much violence in big cities
2. Do you like the city you live in now?	☐	☐	
3. Is there a problem with small towns disappearing in your country?	☐	☐	
4. Are immigrants and ethnic minorities treated well in your country?	☐	☐	
5. Do you think too many emigration to big city is the reason of pollution & social evils			
6.			

B | Interview a partner using the questionnaire from exercise **A**. Use the language from this lesson to ask about reasons and keep the conversation going.

— Do many people emigrate from your country?
— Yes, they do.
— What are the reasons for that?
— Well, there are not enough jobs right now. Also, there is a lot of violence in the big cities, so people want to leave.

SPEAKING

Discussing Case Studies

A | Read these case studies about people who want to emigrate to other countries. Underline or highlight the most important information for each person.

Case Study 1 Ayu

Ayu lives in a village in Indonesia. She has two young children. Her husband died last year, and now she and her children live on her parents' farm. Five years ago, Ayu's friend Melati got a job in Singapore. Melati works as a housemaid, and she has saved enough money to send her son to college. She called Ayu to tell her that she knows another family that is looking for a housemaid. She is sure the family would hire Ayu. Ayu could save a lot of money if she took the job, but housemaids in Singapore can't get visas for their children.

Case Study 2 Luka

Luka is 30 years old, and lives in Zagreb, Croatia. He was trained as an architect, but he hasn't been able to find a job in his field since he graduated from the technical university. One of his former professors told him that there are not enough architects in New Zealand. Luka's girlfriend Maya, who is a nurse, thinks they should get married and emigrate to New Zealand. Luka really wants to work as an architect, but he is worried about his father, who is in very poor health.

Case Study 3 Ibrahim

Ibrahim is a 16-year-old boy from Nigeria. Five years ago, he was playing soccer in the street with his friends, and a foreign coach saw how well he was playing. Now the coach wants to take Ibrahim to France. He says he can get Ibrahim a visa and help him continue his soccer training in Paris. The coach says that if Ibrahim plays well enough, he can get a position on a European soccer team and make a lot of money. Ibrahim has always dreamed of playing for a foreign team, but his parents don't know whether they can trust the coach. His parents are worried that the coach isn't telling the truth.

B | **Collaboration.** With a partner, make notes in a T-chart like the one to the right for each person. List reasons to stay or leave for each person.

Reasons to stay	Reasons to leave
1 - can't get visas for their children	- got job → make money
2 - his father is poor health	- got job (not enough architects in New Zealand)
3 - his parents don't trust the coach	- can play soccer in European soccer team

C | **Discussion.** Form a group with another pair of students. Share your notes, and then agree on whether each person should stay or leave. Use expressions from page 50 when asking about reasons.

D | **Presentation.** Explain your group's decisions to the class.

LESSON A AND B VIEWING

Turkish Germany

Turkish family arriving at the train station in Munich.

Before Viewing

A | Read about Germany's guest worker program. Then look at the information in the line graph.

Moving To Germany

During World War II, many Germans emigrated from their country. Then after the war, when the country was rebuilding and the economy was growing, there was a shortage of workers. So Germany made agreements with several countries to allow workers, mostly men, to live in the country for two years and work at industrial jobs. After two years, the men were expected to return to their home countries, which included Italy, Spain, Greece, and Turkey.

The guest worker program began in 1955 and ended in 1973, when Germany's economic growth slowed. In contrast to the economy, the number of foreigners in Germany continued to grow as family members joined the workers. A new agreement among European Union countries also allowed Italians to enter Germany without any special permission. In addition, a second generation had been born, and those babies were still foreigners according to German law.

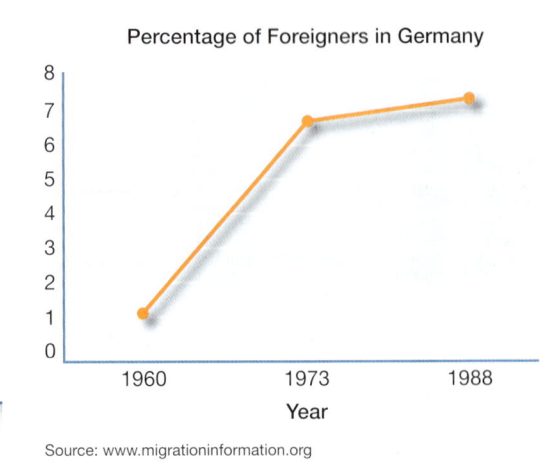

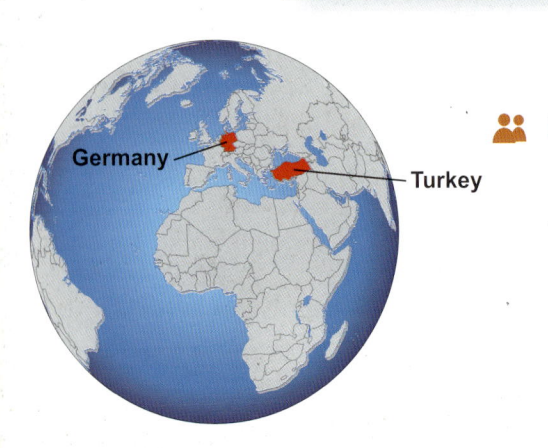

Percentage of Foreigners in Germany

Source: www.migrationinformation.org

B | **Understanding Visuals.** With a partner, talk about the information shown in the line graph. *The x axis shows the year and the y axis shows the percentage of foreign immigrants. (See page 216 in the Independent Student Handbook for more information on understanding graphs.)*

1. What was the immigration trend between 1960 and 1988?
2. Do you think this trend has continued in Germany? Why, or why not?
3. What do the people who immigrated to Germany during the guest worker program have in common with other people you learned about in Lesson A of the unit?

52 | UNIT 3

C | Complete each sentence with *enough, not enough,* or *too.*

1. The guest worker program began when there were ____not enough____ workers in Germany.
2. In 1955, German companies had ____enough____ money to pay foreign workers.
3. The government expected the guest workers to be temporary residents, so from the government's point of view, some of the workers stayed in Germany ____too____ long.
4. By 1973, there was ____enough____ economic growth to support the program.

A Turkish family taking a walk in Berlin.

While Viewing

A | Watch the video and check (✔) the aspects of Turkish culture that you see.

❏ food   ❏ music   ❏ clothing   ❏ religion   ✔ language   ❏ art   ❏ other *public school*

B | Watch the video again and pay close attention to the part about the Rixdorfer Elementary School. Then circle the correct word or phrase in each sentence.

1. The Turkish and German children are (together/separated).
2. The price there is (higher/lower) than average.
3. The teachers use (one language/two languages).
4. The success rate at the school is (higher/lower) than average.

After Viewing

Critical Thinking Focus: Analyzing Information

While you listen to or view information, it's important to think about what you're hearing and seeing. For example, you might want to compare it with other information you've heard on the same topic. Or you may need to make inferences about the information you're *not* hearing in order to "fill in the blanks."

Critical Thinking. Discuss the issues below with two or three other students.

1. The video doesn't address specific problems faced by the Turkish community in Germany, but it does tell us that, *"Turkish fears grew when the Berlin Wall fell and the government focused on reunification rather than the needs of minorities."* Discuss the kinds of problems you think the Turkish people and other immigrant groups in Germany might face.
2. The woman who speaks in the video talks about the children at the Rixdorfer Elementary School. She says, *"They don't see the difference between the Turkish and the German, and so they have no problems with foreigners. They are not foreigners. They are kids."* Do you think bilingual and bi-cultural schools are an effective solution to Germany's problems?

LESSON B — BUILDING VOCABULARY

A | Write the word from the box that can replace the words in parentheses. These are words you will hear and use in Lesson B. Use your dictionary to help you. Then listen and check your answers.

assimilate	settle	ancestors	minority	attitude
generation	positive	ethnic	discrimination	retain

1. My last name is Petrov. My _____ (grandparents and great-grandparents) were from Russia.
2. The Aborigines are a _____ (small group of people) in Australia.
3. Most of the younger _____ (people born in the same period of time) in my country can speak English well.
4. Carlos had a very _____ (good) experience studying in Beijing. He said his classmates were really friendly.
5. One day, I would like to _____ (make a permanent home) in Canada. It's a beautiful country with lots of opportunities.
6. My family came from Sweden a very long time ago, but we still _____ (keep) some of the old Swedish customs.
7. Malaysia is the home of many different _____ (racial and cultural) groups, including Malays, Chinese, Indians, and tribal people.
8. Some immigrants think that they should try very hard not to _____ (adopt the customs of new culture) or learn the language of the country they are living in.
9. In the past, there was a lot of _____ (unfair treatment) towards people from the southern part of my country. Today, the problem isn't as bad.
10. My grandmother didn't like foreigners, but then she had a doctor from India and she really liked him. That changed her _____ (way of thinking) about them completely!

B | **Self Reflection.** Answer the questions in your notebook with your own ideas. Then discuss your answers with a partner. Use the vocabulary from exercise **A** in your answers.

1. Have you ever changed your *attitude* about anything? How did your *attitude* change? Why?
2. Where are your *ancestors* from? What do you know about them?
3. List three ways the older *generation* is different from the younger *generation* in your country.
4. Has your family *retained* any traditions and customs? Explain.
5. What ethnic *minorities* are there in your country? How are they treated? Do people *discriminate* against them?

USING VOCABULARY

A | Read the information about one group of immigrants. Your partner will read about the other group.

B | **Note-Taking.** Take turns telling your partner about the information you read. Take notes as you listen.

Student A — Hmong Americans

The Hmong are an ethnic minority from Vietnam, Laos, and Thailand. In the 1970s, after the war between the U.S. and Vietnam, many Hmong were forced to leave their homes, and a large number of them emigrated to the U.S. to settle permanently. The Hmong were mostly uneducated farmers in their native countries. When they emigrated to the U.S., many of them settled together in small towns and started vegetable farms. They retained many of their native customs and did not learn much English. The Hmong people mainly kept to themselves, but many of the local people did not like having them in their communities. Today, most young Hmong-Americans are bilingual and well educated, but their parents make sure the family retains the traditional culture and customs.

Student B — Japanese Brazilians

The first Japanese immigrants came to Brazil in 1908, and today Brazil has the largest Japanese community outside of Japan. Japanese immigrants came to work on coffee farms across Brazil. They planned to stay only a few years, make money, and then go home. However, very few returned to Japan. During the 1940s, there were many laws that restricted the activities and freedom of Japanese Brazilians. Life improved for the Japanese Brazilians in the 1970s. They moved into new fields of business and became very successful. Today, only the oldest people in the community still speak Japanese, and the majority of the youngest generation are of mixed race.

C | **Using a Graphic Organizer.** Discuss the questions below with your partner. Then create a Venn diagram comparing the Hmong Americans and the Japanese Brazilians. (See page 214 of the Independent Student Handbook for more information on Venn diagrams.)

1. How are the Hmong Americans and the Japanese Brazilians similar?
2. How are they different?

D | **Critical Thinking.** Discuss the questions below with your partner. Refer to the information in your Venn diagram from exercise **C** to help you.

1. Which group do you think had a more positive experience in their new country?
2. How much did each group assimilate into their new culture?
3. Do you think both groups of people were successful in their new countries? Why, or why not?

LESSON B | DEVELOPING LISTENING SKILLS

A foreign worker stacks fish traps near the Burj a Arab hotel in Dubai.

Emigrants leave Djakarta to resettle on less developed islands.

Before Listening

Prior Knowledge. Discuss the questions with a partner.

1. Do you know someone who has gone to live abroad? Why did that person go?
2. Did that person stay there or return home? Why?
3. Do you think that person was successful? Why, or why not?

Listening: A Small Group Discussion

A | Using a Graphic Organizer. Listen to a teacher give a discussion assignment. In your notebook, make a chart like the one below. Complete the left-hand column in the chart. (*See pages 214-215 of the Independent Student Handbook for information on using graphic organizers.*)

	Josh's	Nasir's	Emily's	Sunisa's
1. Who emigrated?				
2. Where did the person _____?				
3. Where did the person _____?				
4. _____ did the person leave?				
5. Did the person _____?				

B | Listening for Details. Listen to the group discussion and complete the chart.

After Listening

Discussion. Work with a partner. Discuss the questions.

1. What was the goal of each person emigrating? Who was successful in meeting his or her goals?
2. Who wanted to assimilate with the new culture? Who assimilated successfully?
3. Do you think all immigrants should try to assimilate? Why, or why not?

Pronunciation

Fast Speech

When we speak quickly, in English or in any language, certain sounds change. Two common patterns in English are:

track 1-34

1. In questions, *do* and *did* are reduced (pronounced very quickly) to become *'d*.

   Why did Patty leave?   *Why'd Patty leave?*
   Where did John go?   *Where'd John go?*
   What time do you wake up?   *What time d'you wake up?*

2. Words are linked together and not pronounced separately. We often link:

   - *a consonant sound with a vowel sound*   your address   six eggs
   - *a vowel sound with another vowel sound*   my uncle   to India
   - *the same consonant sound*   a big girl   that town

track 1-35

A | Listen to five sentences from the listening passage. Write down each sentence.

1. _____
2. _____
3. _____
4. _____
5. _____

B | Circle the places where *do* and *did* are reduced. Underline the places where words can be linked together.

C | Practice saying the sentences from exercise **A** with a partner. Link and reduce the sounds.

LESSON B: EXPLORING SPOKEN ENGLISH

Grammar

Using the Past Continuous Tense

We use the past continuous tense to talk about something that was in progress at a certain time in the past.

*In 1990, my family **was living** in Tokyo.*

We can also use the past continuous with *while* to talk about two things that were happening at the same time in the past.

*My brother **was working** full time **while** he **was earning** his college degree.*
***While** I **was trying** to study, my roommate **was talking** on the phone.*

The past continuous can be used to provide background information or "set the scene" for a story.

*Everyone knew that a war **was coming**, and my grandparents were lucky to get out.*

A | Practice asking and answering the questions below with a partner. Use complete sentences in your answers.

> At 9:30 last night, I was . . .

1. What were you doing last night at 9:30?
2. What were you thinking about while you were coming to class today?
3. Where did your family live when you were growing up?
4. What was happening in your country the year you were born?
5. At the age of 10, what were you planning to do later in life?
6. Where were your grandparents living the year your mother/father was born?

B | The following sentences describe two things that were happening at the same time in the past. Complete each sentence with the past continuous and your own ideas.

1. While you __were having fun at the beach__ yesterday, I was studying for the English test.
2. While your ancestors were living in a castle, my ancestors _____.
3. While the first astronaut was walking on the moon, _____.
4. Last night, I _____ while my friend _____.
5. Your grandparents were working on a farm while my grandparents _____.
6. While we _____ last weekend, our teacher _____.

Language Function

Telling a Personal History

A personal history is a story with information about significant events in our lives or in the lives of people we know. We often talk about our own personal history in social situations or in more formal situations such as job or college interviews.

A | **Brainstorming.** Make a list of people you know who have emigrated to another country or immigrated to your country. Your list can include family members, friends, or yourself.

B | **Using a Graphic Organizer.** Choose one of the people from your list and write notes about the person that answer the questions in the graphic organizer below. Think about the type of information the students talked about on page 56.

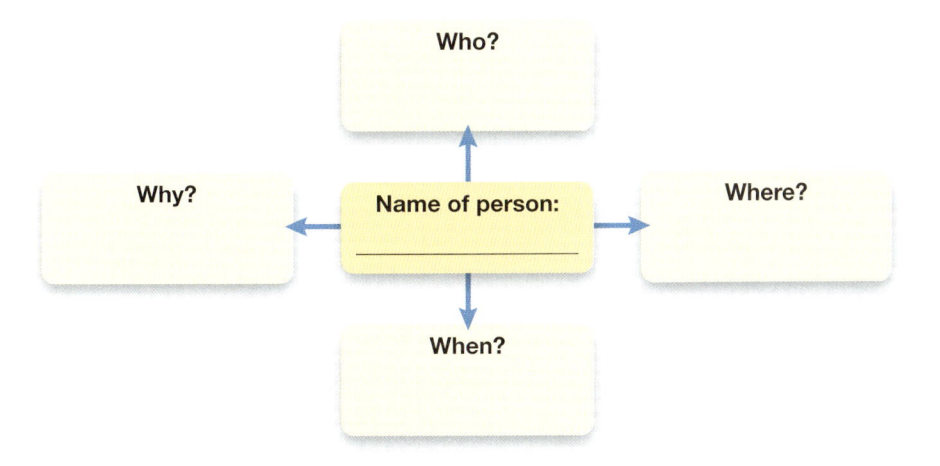

Who?

Why?

Name of person: _____

Where?

When?

Storytelling Tips

Including smaller details will help make your story "come alive" and be more interesting for your listener. Here are some types of details you might include.

People's likes and dislikes
My dad and uncle were crazy about baseball.

People's funny or interesting habits
My sister cried every time my father left.

Specific details about the situation
When we drove my sister to the airport it was snowing.

C | Look back at your graphic organizer in exercise **B**. Add some details to your story to make it come alive.

D | **Presentation.** Tell your story to your group. Use the notes from your graphic organizer to help you. Allow time to ask and answer questions about each other's stories.

Student to Student: Asking Sensitive Questions

When asking a question about information that may be very personal or sensitive, you can soften your question with these expressions:

I hope this isn't too personal, but . . . ?
Do you mind if I ask . . . ?
Would you mind telling me . . . ?
Can I ask . . . ?

UNIT 3

ENGAGE: Giving a Group Presentation

You are going to give a group presentation to the class about a group of people who moved to a new place abroad, or to another region of their own country (for example, Turkish people in Germany). You should include pictures, graphs, or other visual information to support your presentation. You can use paper, the board, or PowerPoint® to help you present your information. Then your group will present the information to the class. Your presentation will teach your classmates about these topics:

1. When and why did this group leave their homes?
2. Why did they choose to go to this place?
3. How much did they assimilate? Why?
4. What is their situation today?

A | With your group, choose the group of people you will talk about. Your teacher can give you ideas.

B | **Researching.** Decide who in your group will research each topic. Outside of class, research your topic online or in the library. (*See page 212 of the Independent Student Handbook for more information on doing research*.)

C | **Planning a Presentation.** As a group, organize the information on your topic. Then practice your presentation.

D | **Presentation.** Present your information to the class. When you give your presentation, all group members should speak. Answer any questions from your audience.

Presentation Skills: Using Visuals

When you use a visual in a presentation, you need to help your listeners focus on the most important part of the visual. You can do this with a pointer, or your hand. Here are some expressions you can use when talking about visuals:

This chart/picture shows (the number of immigrants in 1900).
You can see here that (some people still wore traditional clothes).
Please notice that (the percentage of Chinese speakers is smaller now).

UNIT 4

Fascinating Planet

ACADEMIC PATHWAYS
Lesson A: Listening to a Documentary
Explaining Causes and Effects
Lesson B: Listening to an Informal Conversation
Doing and Discussing Internet Research

Think and Discuss

1. Look at the photo. Would you like to visit this place? Why? Why not?
2. Why do people like to visit natural places?

New Zealand's Tongagiro National Park has three active volcanoes and an ancient native forest.

Exploring the Theme:
Fascinating Planet

Look at the photos and read the captions. Then discuss the questions.

1. What do you find interesting or surprising about the information on these pages?
2. What do you think the environment and climate are like in the Tsingy?
3. What are some of the national parks in your country? What makes them special?

Rare Species in the Tsingy

The dry upper parts of the Tsingy are the favorite places for some animals. This dragonfly is cooling itself.

The *Pachypodium* plant does not need much water, so it does well in the highest regions of the Tsingy.

The Tsingy de Bemaraha National Park in Madagascar

The Tsingy de Bemaraha National Park in Madagascar is a very unusual place. Its sharp pointed peaks are made from eroded limestone. The high peaks and low canyons here are home to many unusual species of animals and plants, such as the white *Decken's sifaka* lemur (shown on the left). Some of the species are so rare that scientists have not yet identified them.

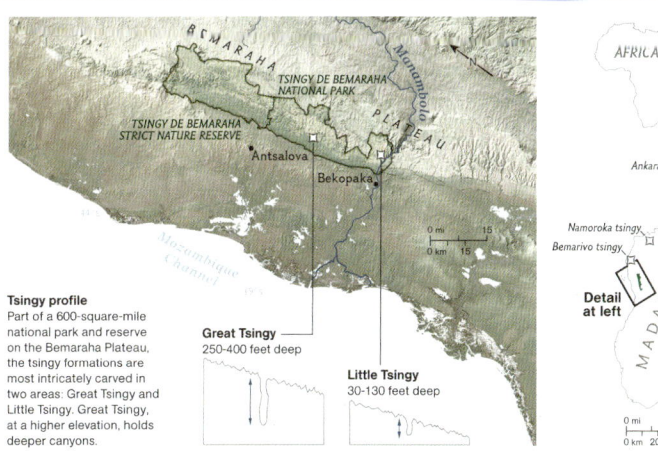

Tsingy profile
Part of a 600-square-mile national park and reserve on the Bemaraha Plateau, the tsingy formations are most intricately carved in two areas: Great Tsingy and Little Tsingy. Great Tsingy, at a higher elevation, holds deeper canyons.

Great Tsingy 250-400 feet deep

Little Tsingy 30-130 feet deep

Source: African Natural Heritage

FASCINATING PLANET | 63

LESSON A — BUILDING VOCABULARY

A | Using a Dictionary. Work with a partner. Check (✔) the words you already know. Use a dictionary to help you with any words you don't know. These are words you will hear and use in Lesson A.

- ☐ crack
- ☐ deep
- ☐ dissolve
- ☐ erode
- ☐ form
- ☐ lack (of)
- ☐ protect
- ☐ rare
- ☐ sharp
- ☐ stone

B | track 1-36 Complete each sentence with the correct form of a word from exercise **A**. Then listen and check your answers.

1. Ancient people didn't have metal. They used _____ tools for farming and hunting.
2. This wall has a _____ in it. I can see light coming in from outside.
3. Sophie can't swim very well, so she won't go into _____ water.
4. A _____ knife can cut into an apple very easily.
5. After it rains, small streams of water come together and _____ a river.
6. I almost never eat sweets, so chocolate is a _____ treat for me.
7. If you put sugar in a cup of coffee, it will _____.
8. This mountain used to be much higher, but wind and rain have _____ it.
9. He's new at this job, but customers don't seem to notice his _____ of experience.
10. Most of the farmers wear hats to _____ themselves from the sun.

C | track 1-37 Meaning from Context. Read about Jiuzhaigou National Park and circle the correct word choice. Then listen and check your answers.

It used to be more difficult to reach Jiuzhaigou, with its clean air and clear blue-green lakes, but nowadays, there is no (**lack**/form) of visitors to this national park in China's Sichuan province. Approximately 2 million tourists visit the park each year.

Water is the main attraction of Jiuzhaigou. Rivers flow down from the mountains, and form beautiful waterfalls. The park's lakes are not (sharp/**deep**), so it's easy to see through the clean water to the bottom, brightly colored with (**dissolved**/cracked) minerals.

Jiuzhaigou is also a nature reserve, where panda bears and (stone/**rare**) bird species are (**protected**/eroded). The trees and other plant life in the reserve are also safe as long as this land remains a national park.

The lakes of Jiuzhaigou get their colors from dissolved stone and minerals.

USING VOCABULARY

D | Discussion. Work with a partner. Discuss the questions.

1. Do you think Jiuzhaigou will stay clean and beautiful with 2 million tourists visiting every year? Why, or why not?
2. What do you think park officials could do to keep the park clean and beautiful?

E | Meaning from Context. Read about glaciers and circle the correct word choice. Then listen and check your answers.

The lakes in Jiuzhaigou National Park were (**formed**/dissolved) by glaciers—huge bodies of ice. Today there are glaciers high up in some mountains, but at other times in the earth's history colder temperatures allowed glaciers to exist in much larger areas.

As glaciers grow and move, they push dirt and (**stone**/rare) along with them. This material, along with the ice itself, is (lack/**sharp**) enough to (**erode**/protect) the land where the glaciers move. In this way, hills can become flat land, and flat land can become holes. Later, when temperatures become warmer and the glaciers melt, lakes are the result.

Glacial ice can become water in another way, too. At the bottom edge of a glacier, (**cracks**/forms) can develop and large pieces of ice can fall into the water below. These pieces of ice then melt and become part of the body of water.

In British Columbia, Canada, a helicopter approaches the bottom edge of a glacier and the lake that it has formed.

F | Discussion. Work with a partner. Discuss the questions.

1. How is climate change affecting the world's glaciers?
2. How do changes to glaciers affect the world in general?

G | Critical Thinking. Form a group with two or three other students and discuss the questions.

1. National parks are rare in some countries and common in others. Which is true in your country?
2. Jiuzhaigou has no lack of tourists. What do you think is the greater benefit of this tourism: the money spent by tourists, or the love and respect for nature tourists feel when they visit the park?
3. The beautiful mountains and lakes in Jiuzhaigou took millions of years to form. How long do you think it would take for human beings to have a major effect on them?
4. Worldwide, there is a limited amount of money and resources for the protection of rare animals such as panda bears. How should people decide which species are worth protecting?

LESSON A | DEVELOPING LISTENING SKILLS

Before Listening

A | Look at the diagram showing how the Tsingy de Bemaraha was formed. Then write the sentence letters in the correct place on the diagram.

a. More water flows into the caves[1] and enlarges them.
b. Cracks form in the top of the limestone.
c. The tops of some caves collapse, forming larger caves.
d. Rain dissolves the top of the limestone and forms sharp points.
e. Water flows into the cracks and begins to form small caves.
f. The tops of other caves collapse, the water runs out, and deep canyons[2] are formed.

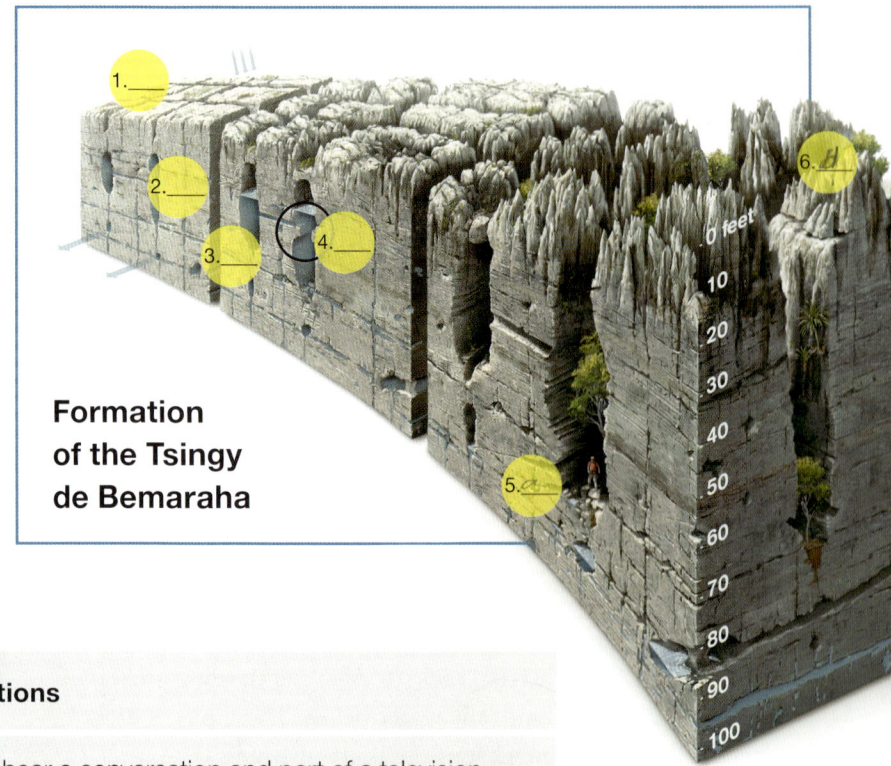

Formation of the Tsingy de Bemaraha

Tuning Out Distractions

In this lesson, you will hear a conversation and part of a television documentary about the Tsingy de Bemaraha. In the real world, there can be distractions while you're trying to listen. A door opens and closes when a student enters a lecture late. A telephone rings during a job interview. Someone talks loudly while you're watching a movie. In each case, your ability to tune out the distraction and concentrate will help you to understand more of what you're listening to.

B | Listen to a conversation in a coffee shop and try to tune out the distractions. Then choose the correct word or phrase to complete each statement below.

1. The woman learned about Tsingy de Bemaraha from a _____.
   a. lecture   b. TV show   c. magazine article
2. The woman's friend asks about the _____ in Tsingy de Bemaraha.
   a. canyons   b. limestone   c. lemurs
3. The woman mentions _____ night.
   a. Tuesday   b. Wednesday   c. Thursday
4. The woman's friend answers the phone when her _____ calls her.
   a. sister   b. daughter   c. mother

[1] A **cave** is a large hole in the side of a cliff or under ground.
[2] A **canyon** is a long, narrow valley with very steep sides.

Listening: A Documentary

A | Listen to part of a documentary about the Tsingy de Bemaraha. What distractions do you need to tune out?

_____
_____

B | **Note-Taking.** Listen again and complete the notes.

- Plants, animals protected in Tsingy because... 1. _____
                                                                                     2. _____
- Name means, "place where one cannot **walk**."
- Walking into Tsingy difficult because... 1. _____ (above)
                                                                 2. _____ (below)

Critical Thinking Focus: Using Graphic Organizers

Using graphic organizers, such as flow charts can help you organize important information in a visual way.

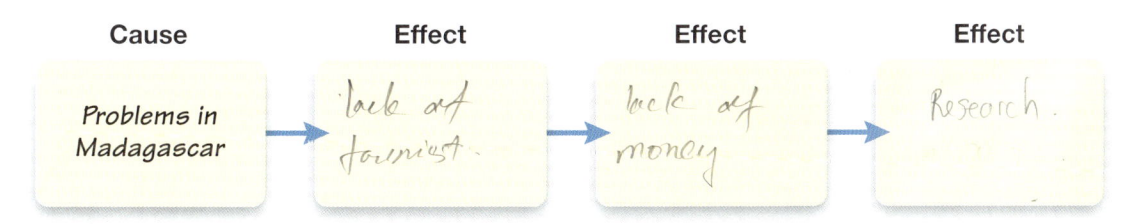

Cause	Effect	Effect	Effect
Problems in Madagascar	lack of tourist	lack of money	Research

C | **Using a Graphic Organizer.** Listen again and use your notes from exercise **B** to complete the cause and effect flow chart above. (See pages 214-215 of the Independent Student Handbook for more information on using graphic organizers.)

An explorer in one of the deep canyons of the Tsingy de Bèmaraha.

After Listening

A | The word *because* introduces a cause. Read the sentences below and underline the causes. Then circle the effects.

1. (The animals in the Tsingy are protected) because it's a national park.
2. The peaks in the Tsingy are very sharp because rain has eroded the stone.
3. Because the Tsingy is almost impossible to get to, not many tourists visit it.
4. The caves became larger because the stone that had divided them collapsed.
5. Because there is little money for research, scientists aren't sure how climate change is affecting the Tsingy.

B | **Discussion.** Compare your sentences with a partner's. Then discuss the question.

1. What do you notice about the placement of the causes and effects in the sentences?

LESSON A — EXPLORING SPOKEN ENGLISH

Grammar

A | Prior Knowledge. Read each sentence and answer the questions that follow.

1. At two o'clock, Olaf was reading the newspaper.
   How much time does it usually take for a person to read a newspaper?
   What time do you think Olaf started reading? What time did he finish?
2. Teresa fell while we were learning a new dance step.
   Did Teresa fall before, after, or during the dance lesson?

The Simple Past Tense with The Past Continuous Tense

We use the past continuous tense to talk about something that was in progress at a certain time in the past.
   *In the spring of 2007, I **was doing** research in Bolivia.*

To talk about something that happened while another event was in progress in the past, we can use the simple past tense.
   *When I **found** my group, the tour guide **was talking** about glaciers.*

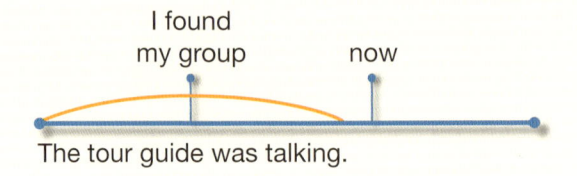

```
            I found
           my group        now
              |             |
    ●─────────┴─────────────┴─────────●
         The tour guide was talking.
```

The word *while* often introduces a clause with the past continuous tense.
   *We **saw** several kinds of birds **while** we were **walking** in the national park.*

The word *when* often introduces a clause with the simple past tense.
   ***When** the lights **went out**, Ronald **was giving** his presentation on penguins.*

A group of eco-tourists in Norway listening to birds.

B | Read each situation. With a partner, say two different sentences about each situation using the simple past with the past continuous.

Example: Between six thirty and seven o'clock last night/you and your family/eat dinner.
The telephone/ring/at six forty-one, six forty-eight, and six fifty-five.

> While we were eating dinner, the telephone rang three times.

> The telephone rang every few minutes while we were eating dinner.

1. In September of last year/you/do research in the Tsingy de Bemaraha.
   You discover a new species of frog.
2. Yesterday at five forty-five in the evening/you/get home from work.
   Yesterday from five o'clock to six o'clock at night/your neighbor/paint the front of her house.
3. Debora/see a bear.
   Debora/hike at the national park.
4. The train/arrive/at seven forty-three.
   From seven forty to seven forty-five/Mitch and Jean/buy tickets at the ticket counter.
5. Last night/we/watch TV.
   The dog/start to bark.

Language Function

Talking about Historical Events

We often use the past continuous and the simple past together when talking about historical events that happened while another event (personal or historical) was in progress.

I **was playing** soccer with my brother when the first man **landed** on the moon.

A | Read about the National World Heritage Program. Then look at each date below and discuss with a partner what was happening in your life or in your country at that time.

Los Glaciares National Park in Argentina became a UNESCO World Heritage site in 1981

United Nations Educational, Scientific, and Cultural Organization (UNESCO) World Heritage Program

The World Heritage program was created by UNESCO as a way to conserve places that have cultural or environmental importance for everyone in the world.

1. 1990 – Tsingy de Bemaraha and Tongariro National Park receive World Heritage status.
2. 1992 – Jiuzhaigou National Park receives World Heritage status.
3. 1993 – Tongariro National Park receives World Heritage status under new criterion.
4. 1997 – Lençóis Maranhenses National Park receives World Heritage status.

FASCINATING PLANET | 69

LESSON A

B | Read the information below about the *History of World Heritage*.

The History of World Heritage

The idea for the World Heritage program was first discussed during World War II, but it took many years to actually create the program:

UNESCO—United Nations Educational, Scientific, and Cultural Organization

History		
	1939–1945	World War II
	1942–1945	The Conference of Allied Ministers of Education in London hold meetings to discuss ways to re-establish their educational systems post-war.
	Nov. 1–16, 1945	After the meetings in London, the United Nations has a conference there to create an educational and cultural organization (later called UNESCO).
	Nov.–Dec., 1946	The first session of the General Conference of UNESCO is held. It marks the official beginning of the organization.
	1965–1972	UNESCO countries discuss a way to conserve places of global, cultural, and environmental importance.
	Nov. 16, 1972	UNESCO adopts the Convention Concerning the Protection of the World Cultural and Natural Heritage.
	1972–2010	Nine hundred and eleven places become World Heritage sites. The sites have cultural or natural importance, or both.

C | Take turns asking and answering the questions below with a partner. Use the information from the chart above and your own ideas in your answers. There may be more than one correct way to answer each question.

1. What was going on in 1941 when the movie *Citizen Kane* was released?
2. When the first computer was built in 1945, what else was going on?
3. What was going on when Miguel Alemán became Mexico's president on November 1, 1946?
4. What was happening when Martin Luther King Jr. was killed in 1968?
5. When Neil Armstrong walked on the moon in 1969, what was happening on Earth?

> When Citizen Kane was released, World War II was going on.

SPEAKING

Explaining Causes and Effects

Causes and Effects

To introduce **causes** you can use **due to, because of,** and **since.**
> **Due to** an increase in tourism, more bus drivers are employed.
> **Because of** the rise in tourism, the company hired more bus drivers.
> **Since** there are more tourists, more souvenirs are being sold.

Note: A comma is only needed if the explanatory phrase comes first.
> More souvenirs are being sold **since** there are more tourists.

To introduce **effects,** you can use **Therefore, As a result,** and **so.**
> Tourists walk on the rock formations. **Therefore,** some formations have been broken and won't be seen by future generations.
> The park charges an admission fee. **As a result,** it has enough money to build walkways.
> The park is beautiful, **so** many people want to see it.

A | With a partner, look at the flow charts that show the advantages and disadvantages of places having World Heritage status. Then follow the steps below.

1. Choose one chart to talk about. Your partner will talk about the other.
2. Take turns explaining your flow chart to your partner. Practice using words and phrases from the chart at the top of the page.

Chart 1: Advantages

- World Heritage status means more people hear about a national park. → More visitors go to the national park each year.
- More visitors go to the national park each year. → More people develop a love of natural places.
- More visitors go to the national park each year. → More money is spent in and near the park.

Chart 2: Disadvantages

- More visitors go to places with World Heritage status. → The amount of trash and air pollution in the park increases.
- The amount of trash and air pollution in the park increases. → Ecosystems can be damaged by human activities.
- Ecosystems can be damaged by human activities. → The national park isn't a beautiful natural place anymore.

B | Switch roles and explain the other chart to your partner.

C | **Critical Thinking.** Form a group with two or three other students and discuss the questions.

1. Do you think the advantages of World Heritage status outweigh the disadvantages? Why, or why not?
2. Do you know of any cultural or natural attractions that have been helped by tourism? Damaged by tourism?

LESSON A AND B | VIEWING

THE GIANT'S CAUSEWAY

Located on the coast of Northern Ireland, the rock formation called the Giant's Causeway is the source of local legends.

Before Viewing

The Giant's Causeway, which is a huge and unusual-looking rock formation made of basalt columns, became Ireland's first UNESCO World Heritage site in 1986 due to its natural beauty and importance as a geological site.

A | Using a Dictionary. You will hear these words in the video. Match each word with the correct definition. Use a dictionary as needed to help you.

1. _d_ A legend . . .
2. _e_ A causeway . . .
3. _f_ A giant . . .
4. _c_ A geologist . . .
5. _a_ Basalt . . .
6. _b_ A column . . .

a. is a kind of gray stone that comes from volcanoes.
b. is a tall, solid cylinder.
c. is a person who studies the earth's structure and surface.
d. is a traditional story.
e. is a path or roadway built across water.
f. is an imaginary person who is very big and strong.

B | Critical Thinking. For each set of causes and effects below, create at least two different sentences with a partner. Use the words and phrases from page 71.

> Because pressure built up in a volcano, hot lava…

> Pressure built up in a volcano, so hot lava…

1. Pressure built up in a volcano. → Hot lava erupted and formed a thick layer on the ground.
2. The lava cooled slowly. → The basalt cracked and formed columns.
3. The basalt columns eroded. → Some of the stones we see today look like steps.
4. The stones looked like a causeway. → People made up a story about a giant.
5. The giant decided to go to Scotland. → He built the stone causeway.
6. The Giant's Causeway is interesting. → Many people visit the site each year.

C | Using the Simple Past with the Past Continuous. Ask and answer the questions below using the information from exercise **B**.

1. What was happening inside the volcano before it erupted?
2. What happened while the lava was cooling?

While Viewing

A | Watch the video. Then fill in the blanks with the numbers you hear.

1. For some people, these ___40k___ pieces of basalt are a natural formation.
2. Dick then tells a story about how Finn was angry with a Scottish giant who lived ___25___ miles across the sea.
3. They say that a volcano made the Giant's Causeway about ___16___ million years ago.
4. Visitors have been coming to the Giant's Causeway and the nearby Irish coast since the ___1800___.

B | Note-Taking. Watch again and take notes in the T-chart. (*See page 214 of the Independent Student Handbook for more information on using a T-chart.*)

Why the Giant's Causeway was Built	How the Giant's Causeway Formed
According to the legend...	According to geologists...
- Giant cannot swim	Volcano made it m.y. ago
- used rock from volcanoes to do	

C | Use your notes from exercise **B** to tell a partner either why the Giant's Causeway was built, or how it was formed. Then switch roles.

After Viewing

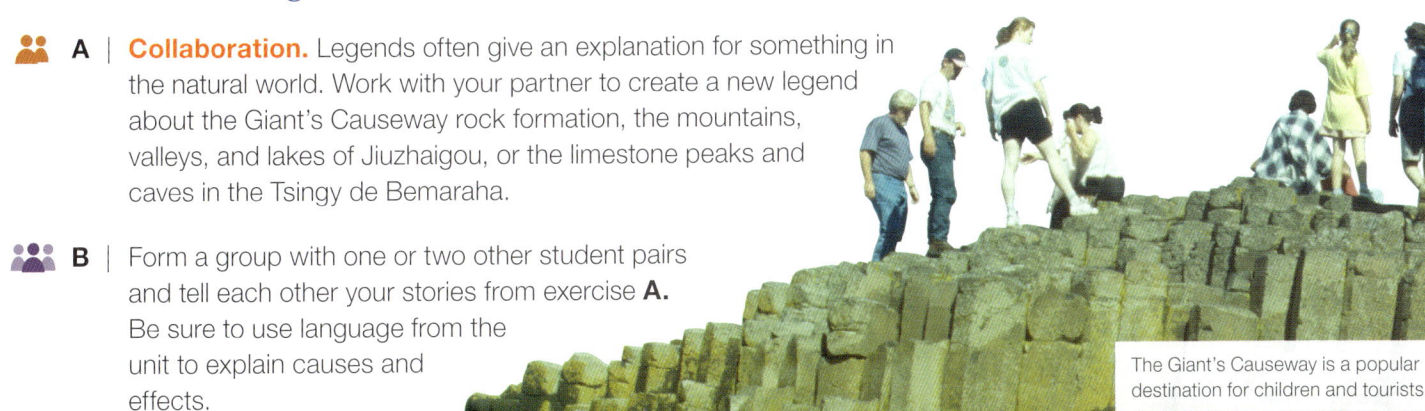

A | Collaboration. Legends often give an explanation for something in the natural world. Work with your partner to create a new legend about the Giant's Causeway rock formation, the mountains, valleys, and lakes of Jiuzhaigou, or the limestone peaks and caves in the Tsingy de Bemaraha.

B | Form a group with one or two other student pairs and tell each other your stories from exercise **A**. Be sure to use language from the unit to explain causes and effects.

The Giant's Causeway is a popular destination for children and tourists.

FASCINATING PLANET | 73

LESSON B | BUILDING VOCABULARY

A | **Meaning from Context.** Look at the photo and maps. Read and listen to the information about New Zealand's Tongariro National Park. Notice the words in **blue**. These are words you will hear and use in Lesson B.

World Heritage

In 1887, a Maori chief gave Tongariro's three **sacred**[1] volcanoes and the land around them to the government and people of New Zealand, thus creating the country's first national park. It has been named a World Heritage site twice—first on the **basis** of its natural beauty. In addition, its cultural importance to the Maori was **sufficient** to earn the park World Heritage status.

Film Location

New Zealand's landscape is varied. It has dramatic **features** such as volcanoes, but also rolling green hills and beautiful lakes, so Peter Jackson had many **options** when he was choosing locations for his *Lord of the Rings* films.

Ring of Fire

The Ring of Fire is an area with numerous earthquakes and active volcanoes. New Zealand sits on the Alpine Fault, where the **edges** of the Australian Plate and Pacific Plate move sideways past each other. The movement of the plates along the fault line leads to earthquakes, and the release of hot material from under the earth's **surface** leads to volcanic activity.

The three volcanoes of Tongariro National Park. Furthest away is Mount Tongariro, and second is Ngauruhoe—"Mount Doom" in Peter Jackson's *Lord of the Rings* movie trilogy. In the foreground is Ruapehu.

Invasive Species

In the 19th century, European immigrants began to arrive, along with foreign animals and plants. These species are a **threat** to New Zealand's native species. Cats, Australian possums, and even rats kill and eat native birds. Plants such as European heather and North American pine compete with native plants. To restore the **balance** of nature and encourage the survival of native species, much work has been done to kill the invasive species brought in from other parts of the world.

Tourism

The most popular ski areas on North Island—with their roads, ski lifts, hotels, and shops—are on Mount Ruapehu. This kind of development would not be allowed in a national park today, but the ski areas date from 1913, and they do bring money to the area. Staff members at the Department of Conservation are **constantly** trying to find **compromises** in park management that will keep skiers happy and protect the environment at the same time.

[1]Something is **sacred** if it has religious or spiritual importance.

74 | UNIT 4

USING VOCABULARY

B | Write each word in blue from exercise **A** next to its definition.

1. _____ (n.) agreement where each side gets some, but not all of what it wants
2. _____ (n.) something that is likely to be harmful
3. _____ (n.) line or border where a surface ends
4. _____ (adv.) happening all the time, continuously
5. _____ (n.) the flat, top level of something
6. _____ (n.) possible choices or alternatives
7. _____ (adj.) enough
8. _____ (n.) important parts or special qualities of something
9. _____ (n.) equal amounts, a state of equilibrium
10. _____ (n.) the main reason for something

Volcanic material surrounds one of the Emerald Lakes on Mount Tongariro.

C | With a partner, choose the best vocabulary word from the box to complete each sentence. Then practice the dialog.

balance   compromise   options   basis   threat

Sonia: Did you know that in New Zealand, they have to kill some kinds of animals and plants?

Nick: That seems strange. What's the (1) _____ for killing them?

Sonia: They're invasive species. If people don't kill them, the invasive species take over.

Nick: So they're trying to keep some kind of (2) _____ between the different species. Otherwise they'd end up with only invasive species, right?

Sonia: I guess so but it isn't nice to think about.

Nick: I suppose they don't have many (3) _____. If they didn't kill some plants and animals, there would be a huge (4) _____ to others.

Sonia: True, but do you think some people disagree with the killing?

Nick: Maybe. They've probably had to make some kind of a (5) _____. They kill just enough of the plants and animals to protect native species.

D | **Brainstorming.** Brainstorm answers to each of the questions with your group.

1. How many of the earth's surface features can you think of? (e.g., volcanoes)
2. What are some things that constantly occur on Earth? (e.g., Animals are born and die.)
3. What are some typical fun activities that people do on weekends? (e.g., going to the movies) How much money is sufficient for each of these activities?

LESSON B | DEVELOPING LISTENING SKILLS

Before Listening

A | Listen and read about a national park in northeastern Brazil. What makes the park unusual?

Lençóis Maranhenses National Park

The name of this national park means the "bedsheets of Maranhão," the state in Brazil where the park is located. From the air, the park's white sand dunes[1] do look like sheets drying in the wind, and it's the wind that gives the dunes their half-moon shapes. However, this park features a lot more than sand. Green and blue pools of water are left behind by the rain, fishermen go out to sea in their boats, and local people take care of herds of goats.

So is the Lençóis a desert, or a seascape? Is it a park, or a place where people live? In fact, it's not a true desert because it receives around 42 inches (120 centimeters) of rain each year. Yet sand dunes as far as the eye can see, along with the lack of trees and other plants, suggest a desert. The park also has 90 residents—people in two villages who change their routines with the seasons. They raise chickens, goats, cattle, and crops such as cassava, beans, and cashews during the dry season. When it rains, residents go out to sea and live in fishing camps on the beach.

[1] A **dune** is a hill of sand near the ocean or in a desert.

Brazil's Lençóis Maranhenses National Park

Two large rivers, the Parnaíba and the Preguiças, carry sand from the interior of the continent to the ocean, where it is carried west to Lençóis Maranhenses.

B | Listen again and pay attention to the intonation in the underlined sentences.

Pronunciation

Intonation for Choices and Lists

When there are two choices, we use rising then falling intonation.

Do you prefer the aisle or the window?

With lists of three or more items, we use rising intonation except for the last item, which receives falling intonation.

My favorite colors are yellow, blue, and red.

76 | UNIT 4

C | Listen to each sentence and mark the intonation with arrows.

1. We have coffee ↗, tea ↗, and lemonade ↘.
2. Do you think the salary they're offering is sufficient, or will you ask for more?
3. We could stay home, or we could stay out late, or we could compromise.
4. Would you rather go to Spain or to Portugal?
5. She's going to Korea, Japan, and China.

D | Practice saying the questions above with a partner.

Residents of the Lençóis lead a herd of goats up the side of a sand dune.

Listening: An Informal Conversation

A | **Listening for Main Ideas.** Listen and answer the questions below.

1. What are the speakers trying to decide? _____
2. What are their two choices? _____
3. What do they decide to do? _____

B | **Listening for Details.** Listen again and circle the letter of the correct answer.

1. What's one disadvantage of the man's vacation idea?
   a. not much to do there
   b. long plane trip from Tokyo
2. Why does the woman not want to go to the beach?
   a. cool weather
   b. too much sun
3. What would the woman prefer to do?
   a. go hiking
   b. play golf
4. What's one advantage of going in August?
   a. low prices
   b. hot weather
5. What is the man most interested in?
   a. seeing different cultures
   b. seeing different scenery

After Listening

Self-Reflection. Discuss the following questions with a partner. Be sure to use the appropriate intonation and explain your answers.

1. Do you prefer to spend vacation time in your home country or abroad?
2. Do you like vacations that are very active or very relaxing?
3. Do you prefer to travel by plane, by train, or by bus?
4. Would you rather go to a national park or to an interesting city?
5. Would your dream vacation be in Asia, Europe, Africa, or someplace else?
6. Would you prefer to have more money or more vacation time?

FASCINATING PLANET | 77

LESSON B EXPLORING SPOKEN ENGLISH

Grammar

A | **Prior Knowledge.** Read the conversation. Then answer the questions.

Makiko: I just got back from Alaska. It was really cold there.
Tim: How cold was it?
Makiko: It was <u>so cold that</u> my camera wouldn't work. I think it was frozen!

1. After she says, "*so cold that*," Makiko _____.
    a. changes the topic   b. gives more details
2. The information that follows the phrase, *so cold that* is _____.
    a. a cause   b. an effect

So + Adjective + *That*

We use *so* + adj + *that* to talk about results or give more details.

> The car was going **so fast that** it couldn't stop at the red light.

In other words, because the car was going very fast, it couldn't stop.

> The room was **so quiet that** I could hear myself breathing.

In other words, because the room was very quiet, I could hear my own breathing.

B | With a partner, think of at least two possible endings for each sentence.

1. The movie was so popular that _everyone knew it_.
2. Emilio is so strong that _nobody can fight him_.
3. That year, food was so scarce that _many people died_.
4. The instructions are so clear that _I can understand easily_.
5. The park is so beautiful that _a lot of people came there for a picnic_.

C | Make a list of eight adjectives in your notebook. Then write a new sentence with *so* + adj + *that* for at least six of your adjectives.

1. _The flower is so beautiful that I can't leave my eyes away it_
2. _The dog was so cute that I wanted to take to my home_
3. _It was so hot that I couldn't go out_
4. _____
5. _____
6. _____

Presentation Skill: Making Eye Contact

Even if you are using notes, it's important to look up and speak directly to your audience. When you make eye contact with your audience, it helps you connect with them. This will make your presentation more interesting for your audience because you are speaking to them.

D | Presentation. Stand up and say two of your sentences from exercise **C** to the whole class. Be sure to make eye contact with your audience, not down at your book.

E | Brainstorming. As a class or in a small group, brainstorm places in the world that match the descriptions below. One has been done as an example.

dry _The Sahara Desert_ Africa   beautiful _Maldive_
cold _Northpole_   mountainous _Everest / Himalaya_
rainy _Changshan_   hot _Dubai_

F | Use *so* + adj + *that* + noun to make sentences about the places you listed in exercise **A**.

> It's so dry in the Sahara that few plants grow there.

> It's so dry that very few people live there.

Language Function: Responding to Suggestions

With a partner, take turns making suggestions about the topics below. Go along with some of your partner's suggestions, and don't go along with others. Refer to Making Suggestions on page 38 in Unit 2 if you need help.

Student A
- Doing homework together
- Walking somewhere
- Talking to the instructor after class
- Buying a new car

Student B
- Getting something to eat or drink
- Wearing warmer or cooler clothes
- Joining a study group
- Taking a class together

Student to Student: Responding to Suggestions

When someone you're talking to makes a suggestion, you are expected to respond. If you want to go along with the suggestion, you can say for example:

*OK/Sure/All right
That's a great idea!/That sounds good.*

If you don't want to go along with the suggestion, your response needs to be polite.

*I'd rather not . . . I'll . . .
Well, I don't really like to . . .
I'm not sure about that.*

UNIT 4

ENGAGE: Doing and Discussing Internet Research

You are going to practice doing Internet research on the national parks you learned about in this unit. You will work with a partner.

When you look for information on the Internet, ask yourself:

1. Do I need recent information?

   The answer depends on your topic. If you want to learn about current events in the world or the latest technology, look for a recent date on the Web sites you visit.

2. Where can I find relevant information?

   Again, think about your topic. General information might be found in an online encyclopedia. Current news stories are in online newspapers. Statistics about a country's population and income may be included on a government Web site. And with every topic, choosing relevant key words for your search is very important.

3. Is the information on this Web site accurate and reliable?

   The Internet provides good information—and bad. Good Web sites often have:
   a. *an identifiable source for the information (Where does it come from?)*
   b. *the date of the most recent update (Is the information current?)*
   c. *the URL suffix .edu or .gov (These sites aren't making money online.)*

A | Work with your partner to find the missing information about the places below online. As you do your research, use the questions and tips above to guide you.

Jiuzhaigou National Park, China
Became a national park in _____.
Size of park: 720 km² *(handwritten)*
Number of tourists each year: approximately 2 million *(handwritten)*
World Heritage status: yes/no
If yes, year(s): yes, 1992 *(handwritten)*

The Tsingy de Bemaraha, Madagascar
Became a national park in _____.
Size of park: _____
Number of tourists each year: _____
World Heritage status: yes/no
If yes, year(s): _____

Tongariro National Park, New Zealand
Became a national park in _____.
Size of park: _____
Number of tourists each year: _____
World Heritage status: yes/no
If yes, year(s): _____

Lençóis Maranhenses National Park, Brazil
Became a national park in _____.
Size of park: _____
Number of tourists each year: _____
World Heritage status: yes/no
If yes, year(s): _____

B | **Discussion.** Form a group with another pair of students and discuss the questions. Were you able to find all of the information? How do you know that the information is accurate? What kind of Web sites were the most helpful to you? What key words did you use in your searches? (See page 212 of the Independent Student Handbook for more information on doing online research.)

Making a Living, Making a Difference

UNIT 5

ACADEMIC PATHWAYS

Lesson A: Listening to a Guest Speaker
Making Comparisons

Lesson B: Listening to a Class Question and Answer Session
Giving a Presentation Based on Internet Research

Think and Discuss

1. What is the man in this picture selling? Do you think he made them himself?
2. Do you know many people who are self-employed? How do they make a living?

A man sells balloons in a busy Hanoi intersection.

Exploring the Theme:
Making a Living, Making a Difference

Look at the photos and read the captions. Then discuss the questions.

1. What is the difference between entrepreneurs and members of a co-op?
2. What are some handmade products that are sold in your country?
3. Have you ever been to a market like the one in this photo? What kinds of things were sold there?

Crowds gather at the Djemma El Fna square in Marrakesh, Morocco for food and entertainment.

Ways of Making a Living

Entrepreneurs start their own small businesses, or make products to sell. This photo shows textiles, which are the main creative art form in Bhutan.

In **cooperatives** or **co-ops**, farmers or workers join together to create one large business. The co-op members also own the business.

MAKING A LIVING, MAKING A DIFFERENCE | 83

LESSON A
BUILDING VOCABULARY

A | Using a Dictionary. Check (✓) the words you already know. Then use a dictionary to look up any words that are new to you. *(See page 209 of the Independent Student Handbook for tips on using a dictionary.)* These are words you will hear and use in Lesson A.

☑ owners ☐ cooperate ☐ wealth ☐ diverse ☑ enterprises

B | Read the article and fill in each blank with a word from the box. Use each word only once.

Agricultural Cooperatives

Cooperatives, or co-ops, are different from corporations or other business (1) _____ in several ways. First, they're made up of members who are also the (2) _____ of the cooperative.

In the case of an agricultural co-op, a number of farmers may decide to (3) _____ and sell their products together, rather than separately. As co-op members, the farmers make decisions democratically. They also share their (4) _____ among themselves. Instead of going to stockholders and executives, profits in cooperatives are returned to their members, who may also share machinery and borrow money from the co-op.

Perhaps the most important benefit of co-ops is the pooling of farm products because large quantities may be more attractive to buyers.

Farmers in agricultural cooperatives are a (5) _____ group. They can be found in numerous countries, and they produce everything from cotton and soybeans to flowers and fruit.

A cheese maker salts wheels of Swiss cheese at a dairy cooperative in Monticello, Wisconsin, USA.

C | Listen and check your answers from exercise **B**.

D | Discussion. With a partner, discuss the questions below.

1. According to the article, what are the benefits of agricultural cooperatives to farmers?
2. What might some of the responsibilities be for farmers in cooperatives?

USING VOCABULARY

E | Using a Dictionary. Check (✓) the words you already know. Then use a dictionary to look up any words that are new to you. These are words you will hear and use in Lesson A.

❏ entrepreneurs   ❏ effective   ❏ poverty   ❏ earn   ❏ assess

F | Read the article and fill in each blank with a word from the box. Use each word only once.

Peruvian Weavers: A Profitable Cottage Industry[1]

In the Andes mountains of Peru, people in the village of Chinchero, not far from Cusco, were living in (1) _____. Their agricultural products—potatoes, barley, sheep—were not bringing in much money.

That's when the women of Chinchero became (2) _____. They started the Chinchero Weaving[2] Cooperative, and they began selling their traditional handmade textiles[3] to tourists. The women may not (3) _____ a lot of money for their work, but at least the money they make stays within the cooperative and within the community.

Starting a co-op was an (4) _____ way for villagers in Chinchero to bring in more money. However, co-ops are not the answer for every cottage industry.

Before deciding to start or join a cooperative, home-based industries need to (5) _____ their situation carefully. If a small business is already doing well, it may have the customer base it needs. It may not want to spend time going to co-op meetings and money on co-op dues. On the other hand, joining together with others can be the answer for businesses that are struggling.[4]

In Chinchero, Peru, children pose for a photo with their llamas. In their spare time, many children make traditional textiles for the Chinchero Weaving Cooperative.

[1] A **cottage industry** is a small business that is run from someone's home.
[2] **Weaving** is the process of making textiles.
[3] **Textiles** are fabrics.
[4] A business that is **struggling** is not doing well.

G | (track 2-3) Listen and check your answers from exercise **E**.

H | Discussion. With a partner, discuss the questions below.
1. Why did the Chinchero villagers decide to become entrepreneurs?
2. Why do you think a cooperative works well for these weavers?

I | Take turns asking and answering the questions with a partner.
1. Who are some of the most famous **entrepreneurs,** and which businesses did they start?
2. In your country, do you think more people live in **wealth** or in **poverty**? How much money do people need to **earn** in order to be considered wealthy?
3. What are some of the responsibilities of business **owners**?
4. Do the students in your English class usually have **diverse** opinions, or do they usually agree on things?
5. Besides business, in what other parts of life do we need to **cooperate** with other people?

MAKING A LIVING, MAKING A DIFFERENCE | 85

LESSON A — DEVELOPING LISTENING SKILLS

Before Listening

A | Look at the photo and read the caption. Then read and listen to the article about an unusual cooperative in India.

Snake Hunters Find Cure for Joblessness

Most people run away when they see a poisonous snake—but not the Irulas of India. For generations, the Irulas made their living catching wild snakes. The snakes' skins were sold and made into luxury goods such as handbags and boots.

Then in 1972, the Indian Parliament adopted the Wildlife Protection Act, and the basis of the Irula's economy was suddenly illegal. Some Irulas got jobs as farm laborers, but many found themselves out of work.

These members of the Irula tribe in India catch snakes and "milk" them for their venom.

The solution came in 1978 with the creation of the Irula Snake Catchers Industrial Cooperative Society, whose members use their snake hunting skills to catch snakes. However, the snakes are no longer sold for their skins. The cooperative has found a better use for the dangerous snakes.

B | **Discussion.** Form a group with two or three other students and discuss the questions below.

1. Why did the Irulas need to change the way they made a living?
2. How were the snakes used in the past, and how are they used now?
3. What might be some of the benefits of this change?

Critical Thinking Focus: Identifying the Speaker's Purpose

In this lesson, you will hear a presentation about the Irula snake venom cooperative. Whenever a speaker gives a prepared talk, that speaker has a purpose—something he or she wants to accomplish. Being aware of the speaker's purpose can help you understand the information that is presented and make a judgment about it.

C | **Critical Thinking.** Working with a partner, think of a possible speaker and situation for each speaking purpose.

1. To give information
   A lecture by a university professor

2. To persuade you to do something
   _____

3. To entertain you
   _____

4. To change your opinion
   _____

Listening: A Guest Speaker

A | Listening for Main Ideas. Listen to the talk and answer the questions.

1. Who is the speaker?
   _____

2. Who is in the audience?
   _____

3. What is the speaker's purpose?
   _____

Indian cobras were once hunted for their skins. Now, their venom is carefully obtained, and the snakes are returned to the wild.

B | Compare your answers in exercise **A** with a partner's. Explain the reasons for your answer to question #3.

C | Listening for Details. Listen again and choose the correct answer.

1. According to the speaker, what does Worldwide Co-op offer to cooperative enterprises?
   a. loans   b. support   c. health insurance

2. Each year, how many people in India die from snakebites?
   a. 20,000   b. 30,000   c. 40,000

3. The speaker encourages the audience members to assess their own situations in order to understand the reasons why _____.
   a. wildlife are being killed
   b. people are earning more than before
   c. snakes are being milked for their venom

4. According to the speaker, Worldwide Co-op has information resources, including _____.
   a. books   b. journal articles   c. a Web site

After Listening

Critical Thinking. With your group members, think of an endangered animal that is being killed by humans. Discuss why the animal is being killed. Then think of another way that people might earn money from the animal.

> People hunt the rhinoceros because they can get a lot of money for its horn.

> Maybe they could take tourists to see the animals—from a distance.

MAKING A LIVING, MAKING A DIFFERENCE | 87

LESSON A   EXPLORING SPOKEN ENGLISH

Language Function

A | Practice saying the numbers in the box below.

Using Numbers and Statistics

200	Two hundred
4000	Four thousand
36,000	Thirty-six thousand
700,000	Seven hundred thousand
1,000,000	One million
1,500,000	One million five hundred thousand (or 1.5 million: one point five million)
7,000,000,000	Seven billion

B | Write these numbers in words.

1. 50,000 _____
2. 3,200,000 _____
3. 400 _____
4. 740,000 _____
5. 8,000,000,000 _____
6. 1,297,300 _____

C | Cover the words in exercise **B**. Take turns pointing to any number and asking your partner to say it.

D | Look at the photo and read the caption. Then listen to some statistics about *kudzu* and write the numbers you hear.

1. Imported to the U.S. from Japan in 1876, *kudzu* grows from large underground tubers[1] that can weigh almost _____2_____ pounds (136 kilograms).
2. During the 1930s, the U.S. government planted _____ *kudzu* seedlings.
3. *Kudzu* was such a popular plant that at one time, the Kudzu Club of America had _____ members.
4. *Kudzu* can cover as many as _____ acres of land each year.
5. Currently, *kudzu* covers around _____ acres of land in the U.S.

An invasive species in the southeastern U.S., *kudzu* plants can grow as much as 12 inches (30 centimeters) in one day and up to 60 feet (18 meters) in one growing season.

E | Write down three "facts" with large numbers. They can be real facts, or made up. Then form a group with two or three other students and take turns reading your "facts." Try to guess which facts are real.

> The population of the earth is 13 billion.

> Hmm . . . there isn't enough space for that many people!

[1]**Tubers** are thick plant roots such as the potato.

F | Read about an entrepreneur who is making a profit from *kudzu*.

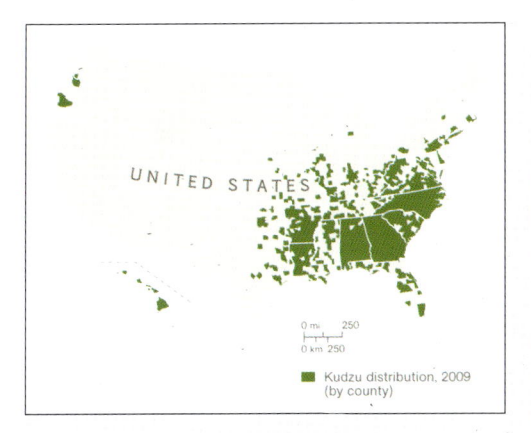

Nancy Basket is a Native American artist who runs Kudzu Kabin Designs from her home in South Carolina, USA. She is one of a few people who see the benefits of the vine that most North Americans hate. "It's very invasive. It grows 12 inches (30 centimeters) every single day, and people haven't been able to use it. But I use it for everything, and people can buy it (from me) in a form that's guaranteed to never grow again," Basket said.

Items for sale at Basket's design studio include her namesake baskets (she is named for a basket-making great grandmother) made from *kudzu* vines and cards and posters made from *kudzu* paper. Basket also makes everything from *kudzu* quiches and breads to jellies and candies. Even her studio is made out of *kudzu* bales[1] — the only such structure of its kind.

G | **Discussion.** Form a group with two or three other students and discuss the questions.

1. What do you think about Nancy Basket's small business idea?
2. Do you think that *kudzu* entrepreneurs can effectively reduce the amount of *kudzu* in the U.S.?

Small Business Statistics

Kudzu Kabin Designs has been in business for over 20 years, but not all small businesses in the U.S. are successful. The statistics in the **Quick Facts** table on page 90 come from the U.S. Federal Reserve Board.

H | Look at the information in the **Quick Facts** table on page 90 and take turns asking and answering the questions with a partner.

1. How many businesses were there in the U.S. in 2009?
2. About how many U.S. workers are employed by small businesses?
3. How many new jobs were created in the U.S. between 1993 and 2009?
4. How many businesses were started in the U.S. in 2006?
5. How many businesses in the U.S. closed in 2006?
6. How many businesses in the U.S. went bankrupt in 2006?
7. Can you see a trend in the number of bankruptcies over the years? Explain your answer.
8. Can you see a trend in new business start-ups over the years? Explain your answer.

[1] **Bales** are large cubes of material such as hay, paper, or *kudzu* tied together tightly.

LESSON A

Quick Facts

- In 2009, there were 1,275,000 businesses in the United States.
- Small firms with less than 500 employees represent 99.9 percent of the total.
- There were 18,311 large businesses in 2007.
- Small businesses employ about half of the 120,600,000 U.S. workers.
- Small firms accounted for 65 percent (or 9.8 million) of the 15 million net new jobs created between 1993 and 2009.

Starts and Closures of Employer Firms, 2005–2009

Category	2005	2006	2007	2008	2009
Starts	644,122	670,058	668,395	626,400e	552,600e
Closures	565,745	599,333	592,410	663,900e	660,900e
Bankruptcies	39,201	19,695	28,322	43,546	60,837

Notes: e = estimated number   bankruptcy = legal inability to pay bills

I | Discussion. With a partner, discuss the questions below.

1. What surprises you about the statistics in the table?
2. How do you think these statistics compare with those in other countries you know about?

Grammar

Making Comparisons with *as . . . as*

We use the expression *as . . . as* (or *not as . . . as*) to talk about things that are (or are not) equal to each other. These *equative* sentences can be formed in several different ways.

Adjectives	These textiles are **as beautiful as** the others. My brother isn't **as tall as** I am.
Adverbs	The large cobra was carried **as carefully as** the small one. Lenny didn't run **as quickly as** usual.
Quantifiers + Count Nouns	She owns **as many baskets as** her sister owns. Pat didn't eat **as many cookies as** Mary did.
Quantifiers + Non-Count Nouns	We sold **as much bread as** we could carry to the market. They don't earn **as much money as** the other workers.

With a partner, take turns making true statements with *(not) as . . . as* and the words below.

1. Argentina/large/Brazil
2. I/tall/you
3. The weather here in spring/good/the weather in summer
4. We/complete this exercise/quickly/the rest of the class

SPEAKING

Making Comparisons

A | Look at the market scenes and read the captions. With a partner, say as many sentences about the pictures as you can using *(not) as . . . as*.

A shopper walks past a variety of fruit at St. George's Market in Belfast, Northern Ireland.

Food stalls in Beijing, China selling everything from seafood and vegetables to sweets.

> The market in Ireland isn't as organized as the market in China.

> There are as many people at the Irish market as there are at the Chinese market.

B | **Discussion.** In a group, discuss the questions for each of the entrepreneurial enterprises from Lesson A of this unit. Use *as . . . as* when possible and give reasons for your answers.

1. Who are the owners of each enterprise, and why did they start their businesses?
2. Which enterprise probably employs the largest number of workers?
3. How would you assess the earning potential of each business? (i.e., Which one probably makes the most money?)
4. Which enterprise do you think is most effective in terms of easing poverty for its workers?

The Chinchero Weaving Cooperative

The Irula Snake Catchers Industrial Cooperative Society

Kudzu Kabin Designs

C | **Presentation.** Take turns sharing your group's ideas with the rest of the class and discuss any differences of opinion.

MAKING A LIVING, MAKING A DIFFERENCE

LESSON A AND B — VIEWING

THE BUSINESS OF CRANBERRIES

Before Viewing

A | Using a Dictionary. You will hear these words and phrases in the video. Work with a partner and match each word or phrase with the correct definition. Use your dictionary to help you.

1. marsh (n.) _d_
2. harvest (n.) _h_
3. legacy (n.) _a_
4. vine (n.) _e_
5. corral (v.) _f_
6. irrigation (n.) _c_
7. hard frost (n.) _b_
8. bumper crop (n.) _g_

a. something that is a result of a period of time or history
b. a sudden drop in temperature that often kills plants
c. water supplied to land to help plants grow
d. a wet, muddy area of land
e. a plant that grows over things and often produces fruit
f. to trap, or gather things in a group
g. an unusually large harvest
h. the crop that is gathered

B | Prior Knowledge. You are going to watch a video clip about Mary Brazeau Brown, the owner of a cranberry company. Like the people discussed in Lesson A, she makes a living by using the resources around her. How much do *you* know about cranberries? Take the quiz below and find out.

CRANBERRY QUIZ: Circle the correct answer for each question.

1. Cranberries are a native fruit to which continent?
   a. North America   b. South America   c. Europe   d. Africa
2. The Algonquin Indians used cranberries for all of the following purposes except _____.
   a. food   b. a symbol of peace   c. money   d. medicine
3. What is the average number of cranberries needed to make one can of cranberry sauce?
   a. 200   b. 500   c. 1000   d. 2000
4. Americans traditionally eat cranberry sauce with which kind of meat?
   a. beef   b. turkey   c. chicken   d. lamb
5. John Lennon repeated the words "cranberry sauce" at the end of which Beatles song?
   a. *Tax Man*   b. *I Am the Walrus*   c. *Strawberry Fields Forever*   d. *Penny Lane*

Source: www.cranberryfarmers.org

ANSWERS: 1. a, 2. c, 3. a, 4. b, 5. c

While Viewing

A | Read the statements. Then watch the video and circle **T** for *true* or **F** for *false*.

1. Mary has always wanted to work outdoors. T F
2. Glacial Lake Cranberries is in Wisconsin. T F
3. Mary oversees every aspect of the business. T F
4. Cranberries are harvested in early fall. (T) F
5. A hard frost is good for cranberries. T (F)
6. Cranberries require lots of water. T F

B | Watch the video again and number the steps of the cranberry-harvesting process in the correct order.

___5___ The cranberries are corralled. *(collect)*
___3___ Berries are knocked from their vines by machines called beaters.
___1___ Cranberries ripen to a glowing red.
___2___ The cranberry beds are flooded.
___4___ The berries float to the surface.

C | Close your book and take turns explaining the cranberry harvesting process to a partner.

After Viewing

A | Write sentences in your notebook using *as . . . as* and the words below. Use your own ideas and opinions.

1. Growing cranberries/dangerous/collecting snake venom
2. Working outdoors at a cranberry company/stressful/working in an office
3. Owning a family business/difficult/working for a company
4. *Kudzu* vines/useful/cranberries

B | **Discussion.** Explain your ideas and opinions from exercise **A** to a partner.

C | **Critical Thinking.** Discuss these questions in a group.

1. Do you think growing food is a good way to make a living? Why, or why not?
2. What are some advantages and disadvantages to owning your own business?
3. Do you think starting a business requires a lot of money? Explain.

LESSON B BUILDING VOCABULARY

A | Meaning from Context. Read and listen to the conversation. Notice the words in blue. These are words you will hear and use in Lesson B.

Margo: What are you reading?

Walter: It's a letter from a **charity** organization. I've never heard of them before, but listen to this: "Just 10 years after our *Schools for Kids* program began, there has been a 27 percent **drop** in the **rate** of poverty among people in the region." That's pretty impressive!

Margo: Sure. I mean, less poverty is a good thing. Are you thinking of sending them money?

Walter: I'm thinking about it. After all, I have a pretty good job, and this is a good **concept**—invest in education now, and there will be less poverty in the future.

Margo: That does seem like a good idea.

Walter: Do you give any money to charities?

Margo: Yes, there's one called Heifer International where you send enough money for a farm animal—like a chicken or a goat. The animal provides eggs or milk to a poor family, and if the animal reproduces, the babies are given to another poor family.

Walter: That makes a lot of sense. Good nutrition is such a **fundamental** human need.

Margo: It is indeed.

B | Discussion. Form a group with two or three other students and discuss the questions.

1. Which charity organizations do you know about? What do these charities do?
2. Do you give any money to charities? Why, or why not?
3. Do you think that charity organizations are an effective way to fight poverty?

C | Using a Dictionary. Practice the conversation with a partner and use a dictionary as needed.

D | Meaning from Context. Read and listen to the book review. Notice the words in blue. These are words you will hear and use in Lesson B.

Title: *Just Give Money to the Poor: The Development Revolution from the Global South*

Authors: Joseph Hanlon, Armando Barrientos, David Hulme

Review: Traditionally, help for poor people has come from large organizations such as Oxfam and WHO, and it has been in the form of complex projects such as dams, irrigation systems, schools, and hospitals. In this book, authors Hanlon, Barrientos, and Hulme present evidence in favor of a simpler approach. According to their data, making small, regular **payments** directly to poor people provides a better **outcome**—in other words better living conditions—than the large, complex projects provide.

Hanlon et. al. describe "**cash transfer**" programs in a number of countries where poverty is a major problem. People in need receive a small amount of money, sometimes as little as five to ten dollars each month, and they use the money in any way they choose. Almost always, the authors say, poor families make very **responsible** decisions about using the extra income, buying more or better food, buying a school uniform so a child can attend school, or saving a little each month to start a small business.

USING VOCABULARY

E | Write each word in blue from exercise **D** next to its definition.

1. _____ (n.) paper money or metal coins
2. _____ (adj.) trustworthy, proper, and sensible
3. _____ (n.) result
4. _____ (n.) money paid
5. _____ (n.) movement of something, such as money from one person or place to another

A father and son in the Dharavi area of Mumbai, India

F | Fill in each blank in the conversations with a word from the box. Use each word only once.

drop	cash	charity	concept	fundamental
outcome	payment	rate	responsible	transfer

1. **A:** Do you take credit cards?
   B: Actually, we prefer _____ or checks.

2. **A:** Are you the person who's _____ for buying food at your house?
   B: Yes, I am. If I don't do it, nobody will.

3. **A:** Did you buy your car with cash?
   B: No, I have to make a _____ every month.

4. **A:** I need to change my Italian money for Australian dollars. What's the exchange _____?
   B: It's not very good, I'm afraid. There was a _____ in the value of the euro yesterday.

5. **A:** Our economy is a mess. What do you think is the _____ problem?
   B: I think we've borrowed too much money from other countries.

6. **A:** You sent them money? I never give away money unless I get something in return.
   B: Hmmm... I think I have a different _____ of charity than you do.

7. **A:** Hi, I'd like to make a money _____ from my checking account to my savings account.
   B: No problem. Can I see your ID?

8. **A:** What's your favorite _____?
   B: I like Doctors Without Borders. They give medical care in places where it's really needed.

9. **A:** I'm really unhappy with the _____ of yesterday's game.
   B: Me too! I can't believe they lost again!

G | Practice the conversations with a partner.

MAKING A LIVING, MAKING A DIFFERENCE

LESSON B — DEVELOPING LISTENING SKILLS

Pronunciation

Contractions

Contractions are short combinations of two or more words. The contracted word is usually a function word (pronouns, auxiliary verbs, etc.). Contractions can be difficult to hear, but they're important because they communicate the speaker's meaning.

<u>There's</u> no hospital in the town. (now)
<u>There was</u> no hospital in the town. (in the past—but there is one now)

In Aceh, Indonesia, new houses were built by a charity organization for survivors of the 2004 tsunami.

Some Common Contractions

With *be*	With *have/has*
I am → I'm	I have → I've (you've/we've/etc.)
you/we/they are → you're/we're/they're	he/she/it has → he's/she's/it's
he/she/it is → he's/she's/it's	They've always wanted to go scuba diving.
Linda's at the library.	
With *will*	**With *would***
I will → I'll (you'll/he'll/we'll/etc.)	I would → I'd (you'd/she'd/they'd/etc.)
She'll tell us when it's time to leave.	We'd rather not have the party here.

Practice saying the example sentences from the chart. Then think of some new sentences with contractions and practice saying them with a partner.

Before Listening

Review the information on page 86 of Lesson A about identifying a speaker's purpose.

Listening: A Class Question and Answer Session

A | Listen to part of a class question and answer session. Then answer the questions below.

1. Who is the speaker? _____

2. What is the speaker's purpose? _____

B | Listen again and write the contractions you hear. Then decide which two words make up each contraction.

1. Hi, everyone. _____ like to start by thanking you for inviting me here.
2. _____ always happy to get out of the office.
3. Your _____ right.
4. _____ worked for several charitable organizations over the years.

C | Listen to the rest of the question and answer session and complete only the questions that the students ask. Write the exact words. You might have to listen more than once.

Question 1: Do you know whether _____?

Answer: _____

Question 2: Can you please explain why _____?

Answer: _____

Question 3: I'd like to know who _____.

Answer: _____

Question 4: I was wondering how _____.

Answer: _____

D | **Note-Taking.** Listen again and take brief notes on the guest speaker's answers to the students' questions.

After Listening

Critical Thinking. Discuss the questions with a partner.

1. Is the speaker working for a charity organization now? Explain.
2. Do you think the speaker is a reliable source of information? Why, or why not?
3. What do you think poor people in your country would buy with cash payments?

The purchase of an animal can improve a farm family's diet and contribute to their income.

MAKING A LIVING, MAKING A DIFFERENCE

LESSON B: EXPLORING SPOKEN ENGLISH

Grammar

Indirect Questions

An indirect question is a question inside another question or statement. We use indirect questions because they are often more polite than direct questions.

When does class begin? (Direct Question)
Can you tell me when class begins? (Indirect Question)

Indirect questions are often in the form of statements.

I'd like to know who makes decisions about money.
I was wondering how communities get things like new schools and roads.

Indirect questions begin with a polite phrase. Here are some polite phrases we use for indirect questions.

Do you know whether people really use the money for important things?
Can you tell me how cash transfer programs work?
Can you please explain why you don't ask people to work for the money?
I'd like to know how people make a living selling snake venom.
I was wondering how people start their own farms.

A | Make these questions for a professor more polite by rewriting them as indirect questions in your notebook.

1. Where does the cash for the payments come from?
2. When will the final exam be given?
3. Are there any poor people in Japan?
4. Why did you give me a *C* on this paper?
5. How much money do elderly people in Namibia get?
6. Who is the director of that organization?

B | Imagine a speaker is coming to your class (you can choose the topic). With a group, brainstorm a list of questions you would like to ask him or her, and turn them into indirect questions. Talk about possible answers.

C | Role-play your discussion from exercise **B**. Use expressions from the box below to show interest in what the speaker is saying.

Student to Student: Showing Interest in What a Speaker is Saying

When you are listening to someone speak, it is important to show them that you are interested and paying attention to what they are saying. Using expressions like these can also help to keep a conversation going.

More formal: *How interesting!*   *I didn't know that!*
Less formal: *Wow!*   *Cool!*   *That's great!*

Language Function: Using Indirect Questions

A | Collaboration. Form a group with three or four other students and follow the steps below.

1. Imagine that your club, Students Against Poverty, has raised $125,000 to help fight poverty.
2. Read about four charity organizations that might receive the money.
3. To help you decide which charity to give the money to, think of one or two polite, indirect questions to ask a representative from each organization.

A Sweeter World
- Gives bees to families and teaches them how to start a home-based honey business.
- Bees can produce honey in the country or in cities.
- Honey is valuable, and people in every country love it.
- When the bees reproduce, the family gives their extra bees to a new family.

The Library Project
- Collects used science books, textbooks, and reference books in major languages (English, Spanish, French, etc.).
- Sends the books to small towns in developing countries to start public libraries.
- Every year, the libraries receive more books.
- The libraries are free for anyone to use.

Business Start-Up
- Helps women around the world start businesses by lending them a small amount of money (about $100).
- Women start very small businesses such as sewing or baking and selling bread at the market.
- When the women pay back their loans, the money is used again for more loans.
- The organization gives advice and helps women with their businesses.

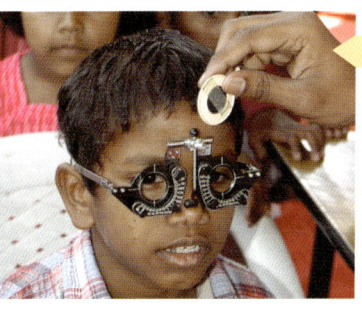

Clear Vision
- Collects used eyeglasses and gives them to people with vision problems in poor countries.
- Children who can't see well don't succeed in school, and workers with bad vision can't get good jobs.
- Doctors travel with the group to make sure each person gets the right glasses.
- The doctors also help people with eye diseases.

B | Get together with another group. Share the questions that you plan to ask each organization and explain the reasons for each question.

UNIT 5

ENGAGE: Giving a Presentation Based on Internet Research

You and your group are going to give a presentation about a non-governmental organization (NGO) that works to help people in your own country or another country. Two very large and famous NGOs are the Red Cross/Red Crescent and Oxfam, but there are many, many other NGOs that are doing interesting and effective work.

A | Planning a Presentation. Follow these steps to prepare your presentation.

1. Choose an organization that you think is effective and is making a difference in people's lives.
2. Go online to find the answers to the questions below. If the organization has an office in your country, you can also call to ask for information. Try to find photos showing the group at work. *(See page 212 of the Independent Student Handbook for more information on doing online research.)*
   - Where do they work?
   - What is their goal?
   - How do they work towards this goal?
   - How can people know if they're effective?
   - What can your audience do to support them?

B | Plan and practice your section of the group's presentation. Your group's presentation should be 8–10 minutes long, and each member should present a part of it. You can present from your notes or use PowerPoint®.

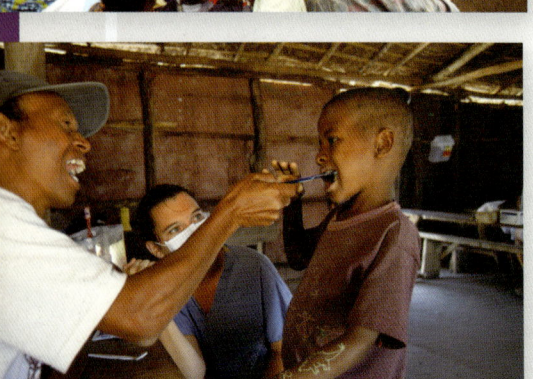

Presentation Skills: Practicing and Timing Your Presentation

Before you give a formal presentation, you should practice it several times, and make sure the length is suitable. The average native speaker gives a presentation at a rate of 100–120 words per minute. It's OK for non-native speakers to speak a little more slowly than this.

Many people speak faster when they feel nervous, so their actual presentation takes less time than they expected. If you tend to speak too quickly, remind yourself to speak *slowly* and *carefully* during your presentation. Leave short pauses between your sentences.

C | Presentation. Take turns giving your presentations to the class. After each presentation, the audience should ask questions to get more information. Try to use indirect questions.

> Could you please tell me how many countries they work in?

Independent Student Handbook

Overview

The *Independent Student Handbook* is a resource that you can use at different points and in different ways during this course. You may want to read the entire handbook at the beginning of the class as an introduction to the skills and strategies you will develop and practice throughout the book. Reading it at the beginning will provide you with another organizational framework for understanding the material.

Use the *Independent Student Handbook* throughout the course in the following ways:

Additional instruction: You can use the *Independent Student Handbook* to provide more instruction on a particular skill that you are practicing in the units. In addition to putting all the skills instruction in one place, the *Independent Student Handbook* includes additional suggestions and strategies. For example, if you find you're having difficulty following academic lectures, you can refer to the Listening Skills section to review signal phrases that help you to understand the speaker's flow of ideas.

Independent work: You can use the *Independent Student Handbook* to help you when you are working on your own. For example, if you want to improve your vocabulary, you can follow some of the suggestions in the Vocabulary Building section.

Source of specific tools: A third way to use the handbook is as a source of specific tools, such as outlines, graphic organizers, and checklists. For example, if you are preparing a presentation, you might want to use the research checklist as you research your topic. Then you might want to complete the presentation outline to organize your information. Finally, you might want to use the presentation checklist to help you prepare for your presentation.

Table of Contents

Improving Your Listening Skills
- Formal Listening Skills   202
- Improving Your Note-Taking Skills   206

Building Your Vocabulary
- Independent Vocabulary Learning Tips   208
- Prefixes and Suffixes   209
- Dictionary Skills   209
- Everyday Communication   210
- Doing Group Projects   211
- Classroom Presentation Skills   211

Improving Your Speaking Skills
- Everyday Communication   210
- Doing Group Projects   211
- Presentation Skills   211

Resources
- Understanding and Using Visuals   214
- Presentation Outline   217
- Presentation Checklists   218
- Summary of Signal Phrases   219

IMPROVING YOUR LISTENING SKILLS

Formal Listening Skills

Predicting

Speakers giving formal talks or lectures usually begin by introducing themselves and then introducing their topic. Listen carefully to the introduction of the topic and try to anticipate what you will hear.

Strategies:

- Use visual information including titles on the board, on slides, or in a PowerPoint® presentation.
- Think about what you already know about the topic.
- Ask questions that you think the speaker might answer.
- Listen for specific phrases.

Identifying the Topic:

Today, I'm going to talk about . . .
Our topic today is . . .
Let's look at . . .

Understanding the Structure of the Presentation

An organized speaker will use certain expressions to alert you to the important information that will follow. Notice the signal words and phrases that tell you how the presentation is organized and the relationship between the main ideas.

Introduction

A good introduction includes something like a thesis statement, which identifies the topic and gives an idea of how the lecture or presentation will be organized.

Introduction (Topic + Organization):

I'll be talking about . . .	*My topic is . . .*
There are basically two groups . . .	*There are three reasons . . .*
Several factors contribute to this . . .	*There are five steps in this process . . .*

Body

In the body of the lecture, the speaker will usually expand upon the topic presented in the introduction. The speaker will use phrases that tell you the order of events or subtopics and their relationship to each other. For example, the speaker may discuss several examples or reasons.

Following the Flow of Ideas in the Body:

The first/next/final (point) is . . .	*Another reason is . . .*
However, . . .	*As a result, . . .*
For example, . . .	

INDEPENDENT STUDENT HANDBOOK

Conclusion

In a conclusion, the speaker often summarizes what has already been said and may discuss implications or suggest future developments. For example, if a speaker is talking about an environmental problem, he or she may end by suggesting what might happen if we don't solve the problem, or they might add his or her own opinion. Sometimes speakers ask a question in the conclusion to get the audience to think more about the topic.

Restating/Concluding:

As you can see, . . . *In conclusion, . . .*
In summary, . . . *To sum up, . . .*

Listening for Main Ideas

It's important to distinguish between a speaker's main ideas and the supporting details. In school, a professor often will test a student's understanding of the main points more than of specific details. Often a speaker has one main idea just like a writer does, and several main points that support the main idea.

Strategies:

- Listen for a thesis statement at the end of the introduction.
- Listen for rhetorical questions, or questions that the speaker asks, and then answers. Often the answer is the thesis.
- Notice ideas that are repeated or rephrased.

Repetition/Rephrasing:

I'll say this again . . . *So again, let me repeat . . .*
What you need to know is . . . *The most important thing to know is . . .*
Let me say it in another way . . .

Listening for Details (Examples)

A speaker will often provide examples that support a main point. A good example can help you understand and remember the main point better.

Strategies:

- Listen for specific phrases that introduce an example.
- Notice if an example comes after a generalization the speaker has given, or is leading into a generalization.
- If there are several examples, decide if they all support the same idea or are different aspects of the idea.

Giving Examples:

The first example is . . . *Let me give you an example . . .*
Here's an example of what I mean . . . *For example, . . .*

INDEPENDENT STUDENT HANDBOOK

Listening for Details (Reasons)

Speakers often give reasons, or list causes and/or effects to support their ideas.

Strategies:

- Notice nouns that might signal causes/reasons (e.g., *factors, influences, causes, reasons*), or effects (e.g., *effects, results, outcomes, consequences*).
- Notice verbs that might signal causes/reasons (e.g., *contribute to, affect, influence, determine, produce, result in*) or effects (often these are passive, e.g., *is affected by*).
- Listen for specific phrases that introduce reasons/causes.

Giving Reasons:

The first reason is . . .   *This is due to . . .*
This is because . . .

Giving Effects or Results:

As a result . . .   *One consequence is . . .*
Consequently . . .   *Therefore, . . .*
Another effect is . . .

Understanding Meaning from Context

Speakers may use words that are unfamiliar to you, or you may not understand exactly what they've said. In these situations, you can guess at the meaning of a particular word or fill in the gaps of what you've understood by using the context or situation itself.

Strategies:

- Don't panic. You don't always understand every word of what a speaker says in your first language either.
- Use context clues to fill in the blanks. What did you understand just before or just after the missing part? What did the speaker probably say?
- Listen for words and phrases that signal a definition or explanation.

Giving Definitions:

. . . which means . . .   *In other words . . .*
What that means is . . .   *Another way to say that is . . .*
Or . . .   *That is . . .*

Recognizing a Speaker's Bias

Speakers often have an opinion about the topic they are discussing. It's important for you to understand if they are objective or subjective about the topic. Being subjective means having a bias or a strong feeling about something. Objective speakers do not express an opinion.

Strategies:

- Notice words like adjectives, adverbs, and modals that the speaker uses (e.g., *ideal, horribly, should, shouldn't*).
- Listen to the speaker's voice. Does he or she sound excited, happy, or bored?
- When presenting another point of view on the topic, is that given much less time and attention by the speaker?
- Listen for words that signal opinions.

Opinions:
I think . . .   *In my opinion . . .*
Here's what I believe is happening . . .

Making Inferences

Sometimes a speaker doesn't state something directly, but instead implies it. When you draw a conclusion about something that is not directly stated, you make an inference. For example, if the speaker says he or she grew up in Spain, you might infer that he or she speaks Spanish. When you make inferences, you may be very sure about your conclusions or you may be less sure. It's important to use information the speaker states directly to support your inferences.

Strategies:

- Note information that provides support for your inference. For example, you might note that the speaker lived in Spain.
- Note information that contradicts your inference. Which evidence is stronger—for or against your inference?
- If you're less than certain about your inference, use words to soften your language such as modals, adverbs, and quantifiers.

She probably speaks Spanish, and she may also prefer Spanish food. Many people from Spain are familiar with bull-fighting.

IMPROVING YOUR NOTE-TAKING SKILLS

Summarizing or Condensing

When taking notes, you should write down only the most important ideas of the lecture. To take good notes quickly:

- Write only the key words

  all kabuki actors men

- You don't need complete sentences.

  ~~In the~~ time of ~~William~~ Shakespeare, women ~~were generally~~ not allowed ~~to appear~~ on ~~a theater stage~~.

- Use abbreviations (short forms) and symbols when possible.

  info information   dr doctor   w/ with   < less than   > more than

  b/c because   = /→ leads to causes

Recognizing Organization

When you listen to a speaker, you practice the skill of noticing that speaker's organization. As you get in the habit of recognizing the organizational structure, you can use it to structure your notes in a similar way. Review the signal words and phrases from the Improving Your Listening Skills section in this handbook.

Some basic organizational structures:

- Narrative (often used in history or literature)
- Process (almost any field, but especially in the sciences)
- Cause and Effect (history, psychology, sociology)
- Classification (any field, including art, music, literature, sciences, history)
- Problem and Solution

Using Graphic Organizers

Graphic organizers can be very useful tools if you want to rewrite your notes. Once you've identified the speaker's organizational structure, you can choose the best graphic organizer to show the ideas. See the Resources section on page 214 in this handbook for more information.

Distinguishing between Relevant and Irrelevant Information
Remember that not everything a speaker says is noteworthy. A lecturer or presenter will usually signal important information you should take notes on.

Signals for Important Information:
This is important . . .
The one thing you want to remember . . .
Let me say again . . .
Write this down . . .

Instructors and other lecturers may also signal when to stop taking notes.

Signals to Stop Taking Notes:
You don't have to write all this down . . .
You can find this in your handout . . .
This information is in your book . . .
This won't be on your test . . .

In a similar way, they may let you know when they are going to discuss something off-topic.

Understanding Sidetracks:
That reminds me . . .
This is off the subject, but . . .
On a different topic . . .
By the way . . .
As an aside . . .

Recognizing a Return to a Previous Topic
When a speaker makes a sidetrack and talks about something that is not directly related to the main topic, he or she will often signal a return to a previous topic.

Returning to a Previous Topic:
So, just to restate . . .
Back to . . .
Getting back to what we were saying . . .
To return to what we were talking about earlier . . .
Okay, so to get back on topic . . .
To continue . . .

Using Notes Effectively
It's important to not only take good notes, but to use them in the most effective way.

Strategies:

- Go over your notes after class to review and to add information you might have forgotten to write down.
- Compare notes with a classmate or study group to make sure you have all the important information.
- Review your notes before the next class, so you will understand and remember the new information better.

BUILDING YOUR VOCABULARY

Independent Vocabulary Learning Tips

Keep a vocabulary journal

- If a new word is useful, write it in a special notebook. Also write a short definition (in English if possible) and the sentence or situation where you found the word (its context). Write a sentence that uses the word.
- Carry your vocabulary notebook with you at all times. Review the words whenever you have a minute.
- Choose vocabulary words that will be useful to you. Some words are rarely used.

Experiment with new vocabulary

- Think about new vocabulary in different ways. For example, look at all the words in your vocabulary journal and make a list of only the verbs. Or list the words according to the number of syllables (one-syllable words, two-syllable words, and so on).
- Use new vocabulary to write a poem, a story, or an email message to a friend.
- Use an online dictionary to listen to the sound of new words. If possible, make a list of words that rhyme. Brainstorm words that relate to a single topic that begin with the same sound (*student, study, school, skills, strategies, studious*).

Use new words as often as possible

- You will not know a new vocabulary word after hearing or reading it once. You need to remember the word several times before it enters your long-term memory.
- The way you use an English word—in which situations and with which other words—might be different from a similar word in your first language. If you use your new vocabulary often, you're more likely to discover the correct way to use it.

Use vocabulary organizers

- Label pictures.

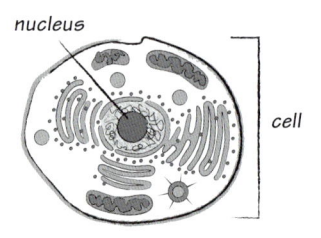

- Make word maps.

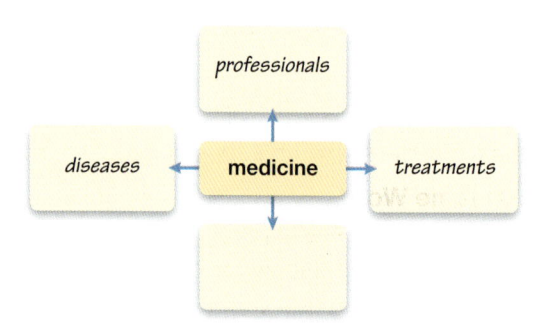

- Make personal flashcards. Write the words you want to learn on one side. Write the definition and/or an example sentence on the other.

Prefixes and Suffixes

Use prefixes and suffixes to guess the meaning of unfamiliar words and to expand your vocabulary. Prefixes usually change the meaning of a word somewhat. Suffixes usually change the part of speech. If you train yourself to look for the base meaning, or meaning of the stem of the word, you can understand more vocabulary.

Prefix	Meaning	Example
a-	completely	awake
bi-	two	bilingual, bicycle
dis-	not, negation, removal	disappear, disadvantages
pre-	before	pre-historic, predict
mis-	bad, badly, incorrectly	misunderstand, misjudge
re-	again	remove
un-	not; the opposite of	unhappy, unusual, unbelievable

The following are derivational suffixes that change the part of speech of the base word.

Suffix	New Part of Speech	Example
-able	adjective	unbelievable
-ary	noun	summary
-ent	adjective	convergent, divergent
-ful	noun	beautiful, successful
-ed	adjective	stressed, interested
-ize	verb	summarize
-ly	adverb	carefully, completely
-ment	noun	assignment
-tion	noun	information

Dictionary Skills

The dictionary listing for a word usually provides the pronunciation, part of speech, other word forms, synonyms, and examples of sentences that show the word in context, and common collocations.

Synonyms
A synonym is a word that means the same thing (e.g., *baby–infant*). Use synonyms to expand your vocabulary.

Word Families
These are the words that have the same stem or base word, but have different prefixes or suffixes.

Different Meanings of the Same Word
Many words have several meanings and several parts of speech. The example sentences in the word's dictionary entry can help you determine which meaning you need.
For example, the word *plant* can be a noun or a verb.

Collocations
Dictionary entries often provide collocations, or words that are often used with the target word.
For example, if you look up the word *get*, you might see *get around*, *get into*, *get there*, etc.

IMPROVING YOUR SPEAKING SKILLS

Everyday Communication

Summary of Useful Phrases for Everyday Communication

It's important to practice speaking English every day, with your teacher, your classmates, and anyone else you can find to practice with. This chart lists common phrases you can use in everyday communication situations. The phrases are listed in this chart from more formal to less formal.

Getting Clarification
Could you explain what the professor said?
What did the professor mean by that?
Did you catch what the professor said about that?
Did you understand that?

Expressing Thanks and Appreciation
Thank you so much for . . .
Thank you for . . .
I really appreciate your . . .
Thanks for. . .

Agreeing
That's my opinion also.
I think so, too.
I totally agree.
You're right about that.
Right!

Responding to Thanks
You're very welcome.
You're welcome.
No problem.
Any time.

Disagreeing
I'm afraid I have to disagree.
I see your point, but . . .
I see what you mean, but . . .
I'm not so sure about that.
I disagree.
No way.

Refusing
Thank you, but (I have other plans/I'm busy tonight/I'd rather not/etc.)
I wish I could, but (I don't have a car/I have a class at that time/etc.)
I'm sorry, I can't.
Maybe some other time.

Inviting
Would you like to get a cup of coffee/go have lunch?
Do you have time before your next class?
Are you doing anything now/after class?
What are you doing now?

Voicing a Small Problem
Actually, that's a problem for me because . . .
I hate to say it, but . . .
It's no big deal, but . .

Showing Surprise
That's unbelievable/incredible.
You're kidding!
Wow!
Really?
Seriously?

Congratulating
That sounds great!
Congratulations!
I'm so happy for you.
Well-done!
Good for you!
Way to go!

Making Suggestions
I recommend/suggest . . .
Why don't I/you/we . . .
Let's . . .

Expressing Sympathy
Oh, no, I'm sorry to hear that.
That's really too bad.

INDEPENDENT STUDENT HANDBOOK

Asking for Repetition
I'm sorry?
I didn't catch what you said.
What's that?
I missed that.

Making Suggestions
We could . . .
Why don't you . . .
I recommend . . .
I suggest that you . . .
Let's . . .

Staying Neutral
Either one is fine with me.
I don't really have a preference.
I can understand both points of view.
I think you both make good points.

Asking Sensitive Questions
I hope this isn't too personal, but . . .
Do you mind if I ask . . .
Would you mind telling me . . .
Can I ask . . .

Doing Group Projects

You will often have to work with a group on activities and projects. It can be helpful to assign group members certain roles. You should try to switch roles every time you do a new activity. Here is a description of some common roles used in group activities and projects:

Group Leader—Makes sure the assignment is done correctly and all group members participate. Ask questions: *What do you think? Does anyone have another idea?*

Secretary—Takes notes on the group's ideas (including a plan for sharing the work).

Manager—During the planning and practice phases, the manager makes sure the presentation can be given within the time limit. If possible, practice the presentation from beginning to end and time it.

Expert—Understands the topic well; invites and answers audience questions after the presentation. Make a list of possible questions ahead of time to be prepared.

Coach—Reminds group members to perform their assigned roles in the group work.

Note that group members have one of these roles in addition to their contribution to the presentation content and delivery.

Classroom Presentation Skills

Library Research

If you can go to a public library or school library, start there. You don't have to read whole books. Parts of books, magazines, newspapers, and even videos are all possible sources of information. A librarian can help you find both print and online sources of information.

Online Research

The Internet is an easy source of a lot of information, but it has to be looked at carefully. Many Web sites are commercial and may have incomplete, inaccurate, or biased information.

Finding reliable sources

Strategies:

- Your sources of information need to be reliable. Think about the author and the publisher. Ask yourself, *What is their point of view? Can I trust this information?*
- Your sources need to be well-respected. For example, an article from *The Lancet* (a journal of medical news) will probably be more respected than an article from a popular magazine.
- Start with Web sites with *.edu* or *.org* endings. Those are educational or non-commercial Web sites. Some *.com* Web sites also have good information, for example www.nationalgeographic.com or www.britannica.com.

Finding information that is appropriate for your topic

Strategies:

- Look for up-to-date information, especially in fields that change often such as technology or business. For Internet sources, look for recent updates to the Web sites.
- Most of the time, you'll need to find more than one source of information. Find sources that are long enough to contain some good information, but not so long that you won't have time to read them.
- Think about the source's audience. If it's written for computer programmers, for example, you might not be able to understand it. If it's written for university students who need to buy a new computer, it's more likely to be understandable.

Speaking Clearly and Comprehensibly

It's important that your audience understands what you are saying for your presentation to be effective.

Strategies:

- Practice your presentation many times before at least one other person and ask him or her for feedback.
- Make sure you know the correct pronunciation of every word—especially the ones you will say more than once. Look them up online or ask your instructor for the correct pronunciation.
- Try to use thought groups. Keep these words together: long subjects, verbs and objects, clauses, prepositional phrases. Remember to pause slightly at all punctuation and between thought groups.
- Speak loudly enough so everyone can hear.
- Stop occasionally to ask your audience if they can hear you and follow what you are saying.

Demonstrating Knowledge of Content

You should know more about your subject than you actually say in your presentation. Your audience may have questions or you may need to explain something in more detail than you planned. Knowing a lot about your subject will allow you to present well and feel more confident.

Strategies:

- Practice your presentation several times.
- Don't read your notes.
- Say more than is on your visuals.
- Tell your audience what the visuals mean.

> **Phrases to Talk About Visuals:**
>
> *This graph/diagram shows/explains . . .*
> *The line/box represents . . .*
> *The main point is that . . .*
> *You can see . . .*

Engaging the Audience

Presenting is an important skill. If your audience isn't interested in what you have to say, then your message is lost.

Strategies:

- Introduce yourself.
- Make eye contact. Look around at different people in the audience.
- Use good posture. *Posture* means how you hold your body. When you speak in front of the class, you should stand up straight on both feet. Hold your hands together in front of your waist, if you aren't holding notes. This shows that you are confident and well-prepared.
- Pause to check understanding. When you present ideas, it's important to find out if your audience understands you. Look at the faces of people in the audience. Do they look confused? Use the expressions from the chart below to check understanding.

> **Phrases to Check for Understanding:**
>
> *Do you know what I mean?*
> *Is that clear?*
> *Does that make sense?*
> *Do you have any questions?*
> *Do you understand?*

INDEPENDENT STUDENT HANDBOOK

RESOURCES

Understanding and Using Visuals: Graphic Organizers

T-Chart
Purpose: Compare or contrast two things or list aspects of two things

Why the Giant's Causeway Was Built	How the Giant's Causeway Formed
According to the legend…	*According to geologists…*

Venn Diagram
Purpose: Show differences and similarities between two things, sometimes three

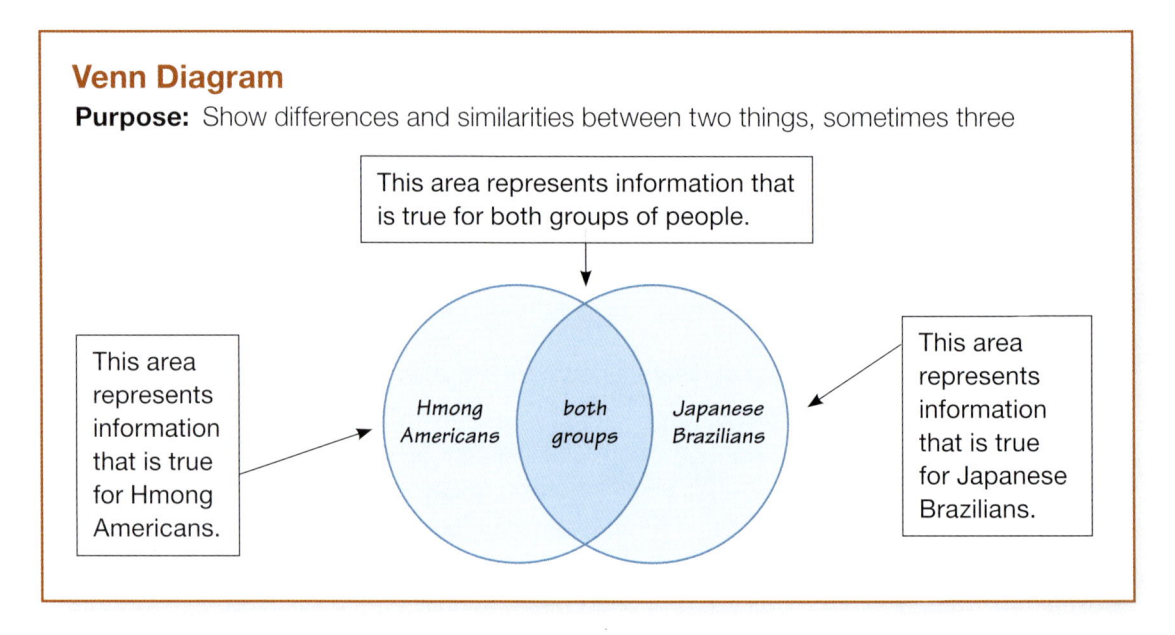

This area represents information that is true for both groups of people.

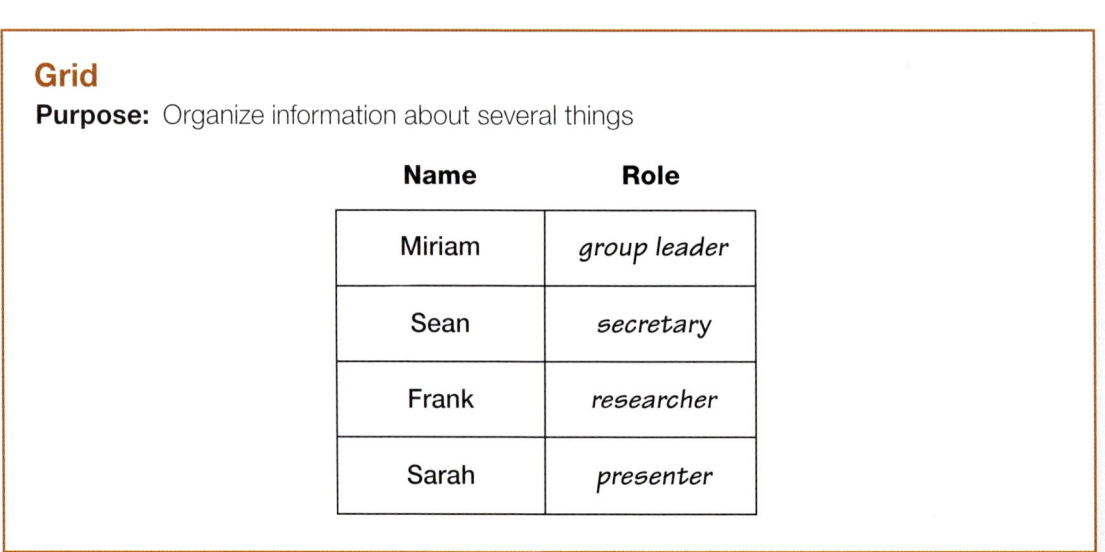

This area represents information that is true for Hmong Americans.

Hmong Americans | both groups | Japanese Brazilians

This area represents information that is true for Japanese Brazilians.

Grid
Purpose: Organize information about several things

Name	Role
Miriam	*group leader*
Sean	*secretary*
Frank	*researcher*
Sarah	*presenter*

INDEPENDENT STUDENT HANDBOOK

Flow Chart

Purpose: Show the stages in a process, or a cause-and-effect chain (Flow charts have many different shapes.)

The Cloning Process

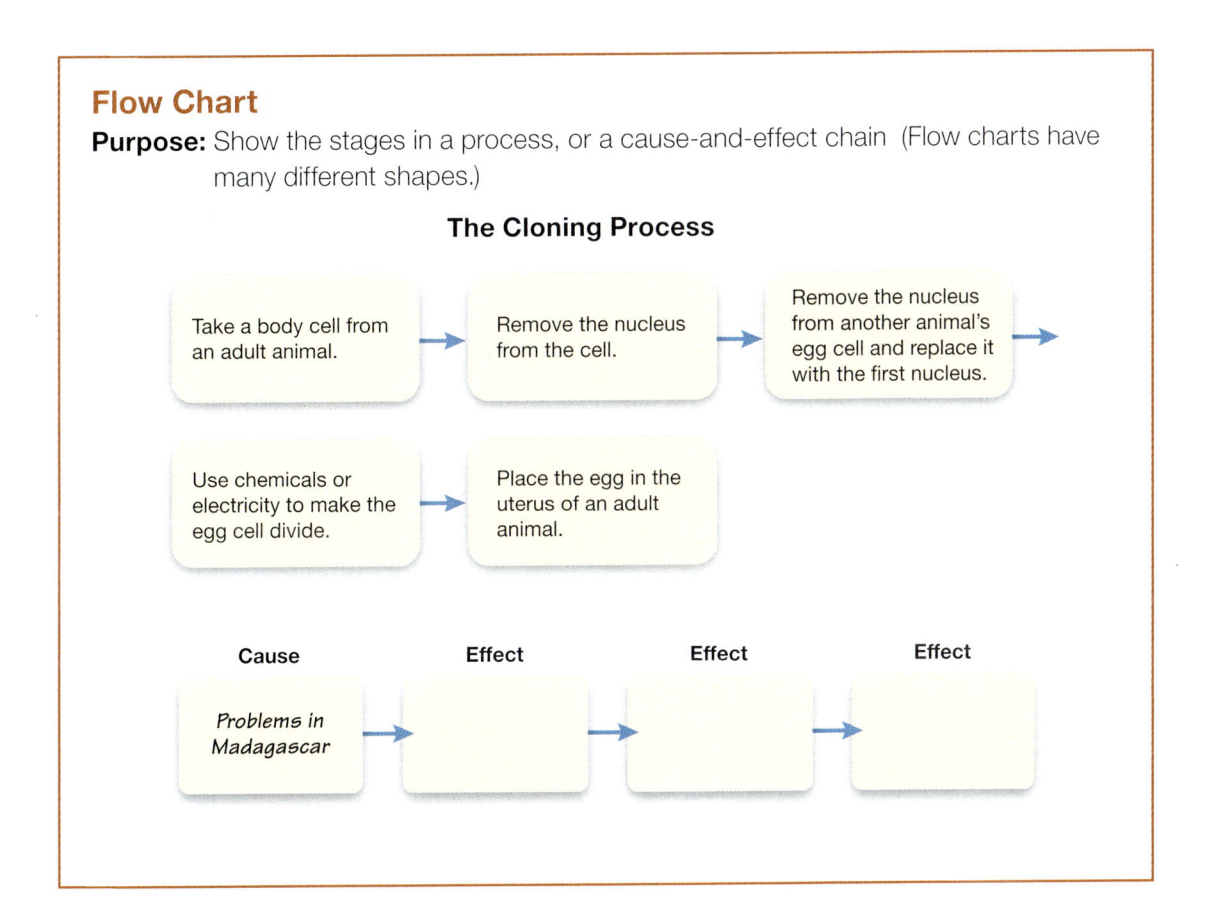

- Take a body cell from an adult animal. → Remove the nucleus from the cell. → Remove the nucleus from another animal's egg cell and replace it with the first nucleus. →
- Use chemicals or electricity to make the egg cell divide. → Place the egg in the uterus of an adult animal.

Cause	Effect	Effect	Effect
Problems in Madagascar	→	→	→

Timeline

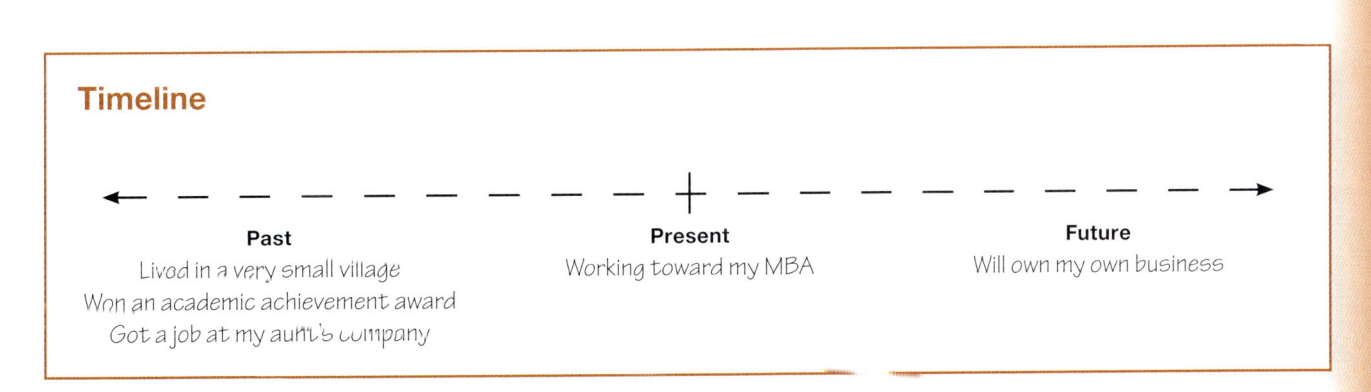

← – – – – – – – – – + – – – – – – – – – →

Past
Lived in a very small village
Won an academic achievement award
Got a job at my aunt's company

Present
Working toward my MBA

Future
Will own my own business

Understanding and Using Visuals: Maps, Charts, Graphs, and Diagrams

Maps are used to show geographical information.

The **labels** on a map show important places mentioned in a reading or listening passage.

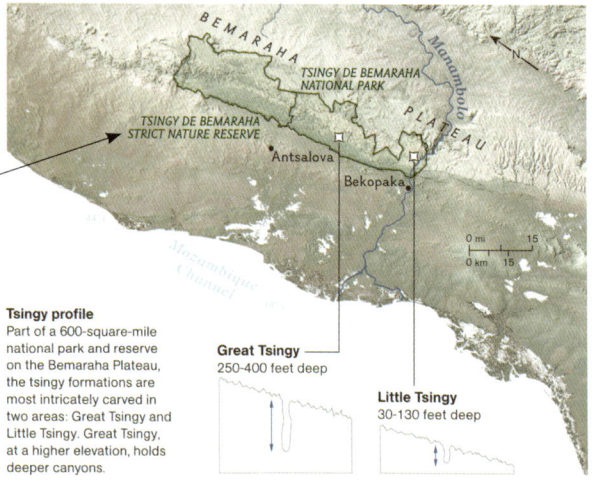

Tsingy profile
Part of a 600-square-mile national park and reserve on the Bemaraha Plateau, the tsingy formations are most intricately carved in two areas: Great Tsingy and Little Tsingy. Great Tsingy, at a higher elevation, holds deeper canyons.

Great Tsingy 250–400 feet deep

Little Tsingy 30–130 feet deep

The **key** or **legend** explains specific information about the map. This legend shows the location of Madagascar and the Tsingy de Bemaraha National Park.

Bar and **line graphs** use axes to show the relationship between two or more things.

Bar graphs compare amounts and numbers.

Migrant Population
- Australia/Oceania 5.0 million
- North America 44.5 million
- Europe 64.1 million
- Africa 17.1 million
- Asia 53.3 million
- Latin America/Caribbean 6.6 million

Percentage of regional population: 15.2, 13.5, 8.8, 1.9, 1.4, 1.2

Line graphs show a change over time.

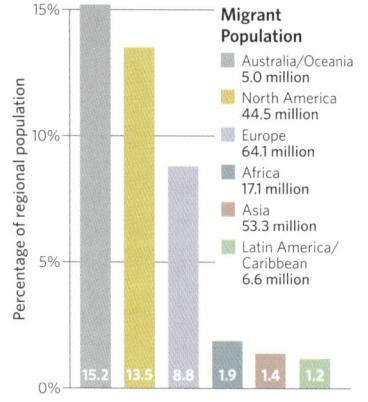

The **y axis** shows the percentage of foreign immigrants in Germany.

Percentage of Foreigners in Germany

Source: www.migrationinformation.org

The **x axis** shows the year.

Pie charts show percents of a whole, or something that is made up of several parts.

Fossil Fuel Use by Sector

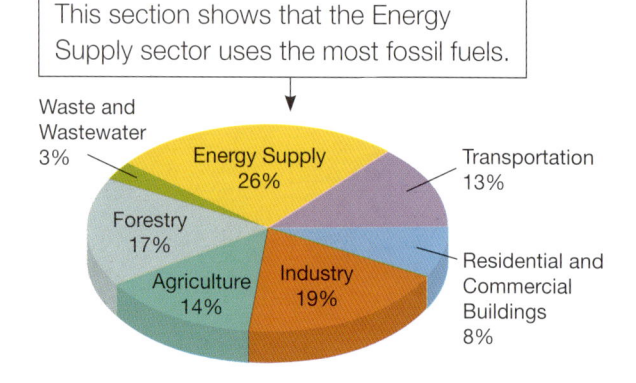

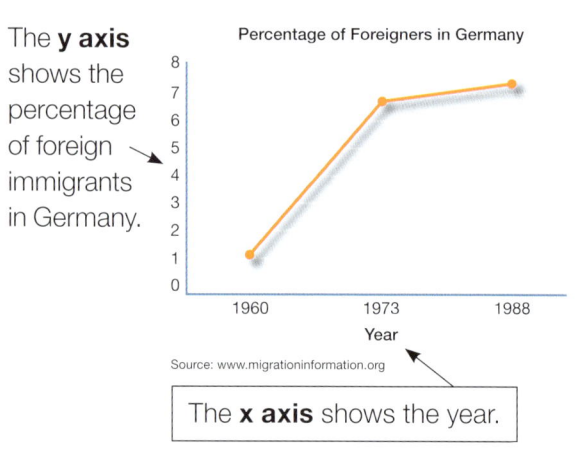

This section shows that the Energy Supply sector uses the most fossil fuels.

- Waste and Wastewater 3%
- Energy Supply 26%
- Transportation 13%
- Forestry 17%
- Agriculture 14%
- Industry 19%
- Residential and Commercial Buildings 8%

Diagrams are a helpful way to show how a process or system works.

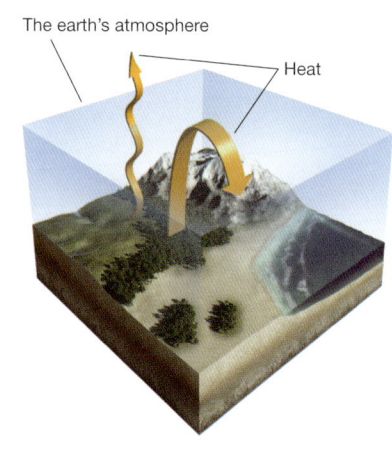

The earth's atmosphere — Heat

Presentation Outline

When you are planning a presentation, you may find it helpful to use an outline. If it is a group presentation, the outline can provide an easy way to divide the content. For example, someone could do the introduction, another student the first main idea in the body, and so on.

1. **Introduction**
   Topic: _____
   _____

   Hook/attention getter: _____
   _____

   Thesis statement: _____
   _____

2. **Body**
   First step/example/reason: _____
   Supporting details: _____
   _____
   _____

   Second step/example/reason: _____
   Supporting details: _____
   _____
   _____

   Third step/example/reason: _____
   Supporting details: _____
   _____
   _____

3. **Conclusion**
   Major points to summarize: _____
   _____

   Any implications/suggestions/predictions: _____
   _____

   Closing comment/summary: _____
   _____

CHECKLISTS

Research Checklist

- ☐ Do I have three to five sources for information in general—and especially for information I'm using without a specific citation?
- ☐ Am I correctly citing information when it comes from just one or two sources?
- ☐ Have I noted all sources properly, including page numbers?
- ☐ When I am not citing a source directly, am I using adequate paraphrasing? (a combination of synonyms, different word forms and/or different grammatical structure)
- ☐ Are my sources reliable?

Presentation Checklist

- ☐ Have I practiced several times?
- ☐ Did I get feedback from a peer?
- ☐ Have I timed the presentation?
- ☐ Do I introduce myself?
- ☐ Do I maintain eye contact?
- ☐ Do I explain my visuals?
- ☐ Do I pause sometimes and check for understanding?
- ☐ Do I use correct pronunciation?
- ☐ Am I using appropriate volume so that everyone can hear?

Pair and Group-Work Checklist

- ☐ Do I make eye contact with others?
- ☐ Do I pay attention when someone else is talking?
- ☐ Do I have good posture?
- ☐ Do I make encouraging sounds or comments?
- ☐ Do I ask for clarification when I don't understand something?
- ☐ Do I check for understanding?
- ☐ Do I clarify what I mean?
- ☐ Do I express agreement and disagreement politely?
- ☐ Do I make suggestions when helpful?
- ☐ Do I participate as much as my classmates?
- ☐ Do I ask my classmates for their ideas?

Summary of Signal Phrases

Identifying the Topic:
Today, I'm going to talk about . . .
Our topic today is . . .
Let's look at . . .

Introduction (Topic + Organization):
I'll be talking about . . .
My topic is . . .
There are basically two groups . . .
There are three reasons . . .
Several factors contribute to this . . .
There are five steps in this process . . .

Following the Flow of Ideas:
The first/next/final (point) is . . .
Another reason is . . .
However, . . .
As a result, . . .
For example, . . .

Restating/Concluding:
As you can see, . . .
In conclusion, . . .
In summary, . . .
To sum up, . . .

Repetition/Rephrasing:
I'll say this again . . .
So again, let me repeat . . .
What you need to know is . . .
The most important thing to know is . . .
Let me say it in another way . . .

Giving Examples:
The first example is . . .
Let me give you an example . . .
Here's an example of what I mean . . .

Giving Reasons:
The first reason is . . .
This is due to . . .
This is because . . .

Giving Effects or Results:
As a result . . .
One consequence is . . .
Consequently . . .
Therefore, . . .
Another effect is . . .

Giving Definitions:
. . . which means . . .
In other words . . .
What that means is . . .
Another way to say that is . . .
Or ,
That is . . .

Opinions:
I think . . .
In my opinion . . .
Here's what I believe is happening . . .

Signal to Stop Taking Notes:
You don't have to write all this down . . .
This information is in your book . . .
You can find this in your handout . . .
This won't be on your test . . .

Returning to a Previous Topic:
So, just to restate . . .
Back to . . .
Getting back to what we were saying . . .
To return to what we were talking about earlier . . .
Okay, so to get back on topic . . .

Understanding Sidetracks
That reminds me . . .
By the way . . .
This is off the subject, but . . .
As an aside . . .
On a different topic . . .

Checking Understanding
Is that clear?
Did you get that?
Do you follow?

VOCABULARY INDEX

ability	14
abroad	44
adult*	24
assertive	14
attract	34
balance	74
basis	74
behavior	4
cash	94
challenge*	24
characteristic	4
charity	94
colony	24
community*	44
compromise	74
concept*	94
conclude*	14
constantly*	74
crack	64
deep	64
defend	24
depend	24
dissolve	64
drop	94
edge	74
emigrate	44
encourage	14
equal	14
erode	64
fascinating	34
feature*	74
female	4
feminine	4
form	64
fundamental*	94
gap	14
gender*	4
generally	4
imitate	34
immigrant*	44
insect	34
instinct	34
investigate*	14
knowledge	14

lack	64
level	14
male	4
masculine	4
mate	24
native	44
negative*	44
obtain*	34
option*	74
original	44
outcome*	94
payment	94
permanent	44
possibly	14
predator	24
protect	64
rare	64
rate	94
reproduction	24
resemble	34
responsible	94
reverse*	4
role*	4
scent	34
sharp	64
shelter	34
stone	64
sufficient*	74
surface	74
temporary*	44
territory	24
threat	74
transfer*	94
trend*	44
trick	34
weigh	24

*These words are on the Academic Word List (AWL). The AWL is a list of the 570 highest-frequency academic word families that regularly appear in academic texts. The list was compiled by researcher Averil Coxhead based on her analysis of a 3.5 million word corpus (Coxhead, 2000).

ACADEMIC LITERACY SKILLS INDEX

Critical Thinking

analyzing information, 1, 2–3, 21, 22–23, 41, 42–43, 47, 53, 55, 61, 62–63, 81, 82–83, 97
    for cause and effect, 67, 72
    for relevance, 27, 31, 207
assessing reasons, 15
brainstorming, 20, 33, 59, 75, 79, 98
comparing ideas with a partner, 15
debating, 20
deducing meaning from context, 4, 14, 24, 26, 34, 44, 64, 65, 75, 94, 204
demonstrating comprehension from listening, 87
expressing and explaining opinions, 7, 13, 15, 32, 71, 87, 93
identifying information, 30
identifying the speaker's purpose, 86
interpreting statistics, 90
making group plan for research study, 40
making group presentations, 40, 60, 211
organizing presentations
    organizing ideas, 40
relating information to personal experience, 1, 8, 12
synthesizing information, 65
understanding and using visuals/graphic organizers, 9, 11, 51, 56, 59, 67, 73, 206, 214–215
    for building vocabulary, 208
    interpreting graphs, 52
    interpreting maps, 2–3, 42–43
    understanding and using flow charts, 215
    understanding timelines, 215
    using charts, 28, 33, 44, 51, 56, 67, 71, 73, 90, 214
    using T-charts, 73, 214
    using Venn diagrams, 55, 214
using new vocabulary, 25, 35, 55

Grammar

adjectives
    comparisons with *as. . .as*, 90–91, 93
    with *enough, not enough* and *too*, 48–49
adverbs, comparisons with *as. . .as*, 90–91, 93
clauses
    adjective clauses, 30, 32
comparisons with *as. . .as*, 90–91, 93
critical thinking, 30
expressions for talking about rules and expectations, 8
for making suggestions, 38
nouns
    comparisons with *as. . .as*, 90–91, 93
    with *enough, not enough* and *too*, 49
prefixes, 209
pronouns
    indefinite, 9–10
    usage, 10
questions
    indirect, 98
so + adjective + *that*, 78, 79
suffixes, 209
transition words, 29
verbs
    objects of verbs, 38
    past continuous tense, 58, 68–69, 73
    simple past tense with past continuous tense, 68–69, 73
    transitive, 38

Language Function. *See also* Grammar; Pronunciation; Speaking

asking for reasons, 50
critical thinking, 8
explaining a process, 29
inclusive language, 18
making sidetracks and returning to a topic, 207
making suggestions, 38
responding to suggestions, 79
talking about historical events, 69
telling a personal history, 58
using indirect questions, 99
using numbers and statistics, 88

Listening

to articles, 86
to class question and answer session, 96–97
collaboration after, 17, 27
to conversations, 16–17, 26–27, 36–37, 66, 77, 94
critical thinking, 7, 27, 47, 67, 86, 87, 97
deducing meaning from context, 26, 204
to descriptions, 76
for details, 7, 17, 26, 37, 47, 56, 77, 87, 203–204
determining relevance of information, 207
discussion before, 16, 56
to documentaries, 7, 67
for emphasis on key words, 36
to fast speech, 57
to guest speakers, 87
identifying the speaker's purpose, 86
to lectures, 7, 46–47
for main ideas, 7, 16, 26, 37, 46–47, 77, 87
making inferences, 205
note-taking while, 6, 29, 67, 206–207
predicting content, 46, 202
prior knowledge and, 6, 56
recognizing a return to a previous topic, 207

recognizing a speaker's bias, 205
self-reflection and, 37
sidetracks, 207
to statistics, 88
for stress patterns before suffixes, 28
structure of a presentation, 202–203, 206
summarizing after, 206
tuning out distractions, 66, 67
using graphic organizers, 56, 67
    charts, 28, 67
using notes effectively, 207
viewing diagrams, 66
to vocabulary, 4, 14, 24, 34, 44, 54, 64, 74

Presentations

checklists for, 218
collaboration for, 40, 60, 211
demonstrating knowledge of content, 213
engaging the audience, 213
finding reliable sources, 212
making eye contact, 79
about a name, 11
outline for, 217
practicing and timing, 100
preparing notes for, 11
reporting to class, 31, 51, 91
research for
    finding information appropriate for topic, 212
    library, 211
    online, 100, 212
signal phrases for, 219
speaking clearly and comprehensibly, 212
storytelling, 59
using specific details, 40
visuals/graphic organizers for, 11, 60

Pronunciation

can/can't, 17
contractions, 96
fast speech, 57
intonation
    for choices and lists, 76–77
stress patterns before suffixes, 28

Resources

checklists for presentations, 218
visuals/graphic organizers, 206, 214–215
    for building vocabulary, 208
    charts, 28, 33, 44, 51, 56, 67, 71, 73, 90
    diagrams, 216
    flow charts, 215
    graphs, 52, 216
    grids, 214
    maps, 2–3, 74, 216
    T-charts, 73, 214
    timelines, 215
    Venn diagrams, 55, 214

Speaking. *See also* Language function; Presentations; Pronunciation

asking and answering questions, 25, 48–49, 58, 70, 73, 85, 89
    asking sensitive questions, 59
asking for repetition, 31
brainstorming, 20, 33, 75, 79, 98
collaboration, 39, 40, 51, 73
conversations, 37, 38, 39, 77, 95
critical thinking, 31, 71
debating, 20
discussion, 1, 2–3, 5, 8, 9, 10, 11, 13, 15, 18, 19, 21, 29, 30, 31, 32, 37, 41, 45, 47, 49, 51, 53, 55, 56, 57, 61, 65, 67, 69, 77, 79, 80, 81, 82–83, 84, 85, 86, 89, 90, 91, 93, 94, 98, 99
explaining causes and effects, 71
explaining processes, 93
fast speech, 57
greeting a friend, 17
interviewing, 50
making comparisons, 91
numbers, 88
questions, 77
reporting to class, 5
role-playing, 98
self-reflection, 77
sentences, 69, 91
showing interest in what speaker is saying, 98
storytelling, 73
talking about rules and expectations, 8, 19
useful phrases for everyday communication, 210–211
visuals/graphic organizers, 9, 11, 51, 59

Test-Taking Skills

checking off correct answers, 37, 53, 64, 84, 85
circling correct answers, 10, 16, 53, 64, 65, 67, 77
fill in blanks, 17, 18, 25, 26, 35, 38, 39, 54, 66, 73, 84, 85, 88, 95, 97
giving reasons, 15
labeling, 27
matching, 8, 15, 24, 32, 44, 66, 72, 75, 92
multiple choice, 16, 26, 37, 66, 87, 92

note-taking, 97
numbering steps, 93
ranking items, 31
sentence completion, 19, 30, 49, 53, 58, 64, 75
short answer questions, 16, 33, 45, 68, 77, 78, 87, 96, 97
true/false questions, 17, 25, 93
underlining correct responses, 28, 67

Topics

Fascinating Planet, 61–80
Gender and Society, 1–20
Human Migration, 41–60
Making a Living, Making a Difference, 81–100
Reproducing Life, 21–40

Viewing

The Business of Cranberries, 92–93
collaboration after, 33, 73
critical thinking, 12, 13, 32, 53, 72, 93
for details, 13
dictionary use, 72
discussion after, 93
The Giant's Causeway, 72–73
Internet research, 79
note-taking, 13, 33, 73
for numbers, 73
photos, 2–3, 22–23, 45, 74, 82–83, 91
prior knowledge, 92
self-reflection, 32
Turkish Germany, 52–53
Turtle Excluder, 32–33
understanding main idea ideas, 33
visuals/graphic organizers
    charts, 33, 71, 73
    diagrams, 66
    graphs, 52
    maps, 2–3, 74
Wodaabe, 12–13

Vocabulary

building vocabulary, 4, 14, 24, 34, 44, 54, 64, 84, 85, 94
    experimenting with new vocabulary for, 208
    graphic organizers for, 208
    using new words for, 208
    vocabulary journal for, 208
critical thinking, 15, 25, 35, 55, 65, 75
dictionary use, 12, 32, 35, 44, 64, 72, 84, 85, 92, 94, 209
to give reasons, 15
graphic organizers, 55, 208
meaning from context, 4, 14, 24, 34, 44, 64, 65, 75, 94

note-taking, 55
prefixes, 209
self-reflection, 54
suffixes, 28, 209
using vocabulary, 5, 15, 25, 35, 45, 55, 65, 75, 85, 95

Writing

brainstorming, 59
collaboration, 39, 40
collocations in, 209
conversations, 39
details for a story, 59
group plan for research study, 40
letters, 33
lists, 78
notes
    for slides, 47
    for speaking, 11
note-taking, 6, 9, 13, 20, 27, 29, 33, 45, 51, 55, 67, 73, 97, 206–207
numbers in words, 88
questionnaires, 50
sentences, 48, 78, 93
visuals/graphic organizers, 59
    charts, 33, 44, 51, 56, 67, 73

CREDITS (continued from p.xii)

MAP AND ILLUSTRATION

2–3: National Geographic Maps; **7:** National Geographic Maps; **12:** National Geographic Maps; **23:** National Geographic Maps; **32:** National Geographic Maps; **44–45:** National Geographic Maps; **46:** Mapping Specialists, Ltd. Madison, WI USA; **52:** National Geographic Maps; **63:** National Geographic Maps; **66:** Fernando Baptista/Sean McNaughton/National Geographic Image Collection; **73:** Mark Snyder for American Artisits Rep., Inc; **74:** National Geographic Maps; **76:** National Geographic Maps; **89:** National Geographic Maps.